# GOLA

## Re-imagined !?! 6.31

Ash Gulati

INDIA · SINGAPORE · MALAYSIA

ISBN  979-8-89929-306-1

"DEDICATED TO SAVING THIS GOLA,
OUR HEAVEN EARTH, SO THAT MILLIONS
OF FUTURE SUNITA WILLIAMS' ALSO,
HAVE A HOME TO RETURN TO"

~ MALINI & ASH GULATI ~

1973~2050<sub>EYD</sub>

*EYD: Estimated Year of Departure*

**NOTICE & ANNOUNCEMENT:**

This version of the Earthizens Revolution plan, as detailed in this handbook, supersedes and replaces all prior versions of plans as expressed in various editions of the book titled GOLA, Re-imagined !?!. It also supersedes any copyrights applied for or any discussions pertaining to the trade names Earthizens Revolution 2050, Earthizens Unity Day – Oct 31, Constitution of Earthizens, Homizens, Earthizens of Eminence, www.GOLA.foundation, www.citizen.earth, or other related trade/service marks, domain names, or copyrights owned by the author and related to this concept as mentioned in the handbook.

This applies to, but is not limited to, short notes, business plans, emails, WhatsApp messages, and any other forms of communication, whether written or verbal, disseminated globally, concerning the proposed plan of Earthizens Revolution and associated work around that plan.

This statement is made on April 28, 2025, the date of reserving the copyrights for this version, by Ashish Ash Gulati, co-founder, on behalf of Malini Ash Gulati and himself (co-founder couple of the GOLA Foundation and the Earthizens Revolution 2050). Malini Ash Gulati and Ashish Ash Gulati reserve exclusive rights associated with the aforementioned intellectual properties of the GOLA Foundation and the Earthizens Revolution 2050 globally, including India.

**DISCLAIMER ( ~ Please Read ~ )**

"Earthizens Revolution 2050" and various versions of the book "GOLA !?!" are sincere efforts by author Ashish Ash Gulati & his family to present re-imagined possibilities aimed at fostering greater togetherness and happiness on Earth. The concepts extended within these books are offered as fresh, humble, seminal contributions by the author, intended for university-level students, faculty, thinkers and researchers to explore, implement, critique, reject, or refine for the betterment of our planet. In this endeavor, assistance was taken from Microsoft AI software Copilot to enhance the conceptualized thoughts, which the author acknowledges as invaluable support in refining and enhancing his ideas.

Given the seminal nature of the proposed research constructs and solutions, the concepts presented in this book should currently be considered for research, critical evaluation, exploration, and inspirational purposes only. They do not constitute expert professional advice or recommendations until thoroughly vetted, which may take years of research following the book's introduction and subsequent retrospective publications. The author and contributors are not liable for any actions taken based on the content of this book. Readers are encouraged to conduct their own research and consult with professionals before implementing any suggestions.

**ACKNOWLEDGEMENT**

Acknowledgments for the inspirational research articles are provided at the end. This content is either an imagination or re-imagination of available resources and tools, aimed at a global solution to this threat. For any missing citations, please contact the author for future versions. The year 2050 is not far, and we have much to do together. Future researchers working on the coined words or unique concepts in this book could be acknowledged in upcoming versions. Please keep us informed.

# Acknowledgment of Support

## ~ Thank you so much ~

Thank you, Raunak!
Your patience, tolerance, and resilience were the catalysts for writing this book, which began in 2022 but truly took shape around October 31, 2024. The term "Homizens" emerged from our realization of the need for fixed norms for discussions following our storming session on Oct 19th.

We are grateful to Raj's parents, our brother-in-law in the US. On New Year's Eve, his mother emphasized the importance of the year gone by, reminding us of the gratitude we owe to those who have done so much already in our journey of life. Her words, "It's the year gone by that we get to see the coming year," resonated deeply.

We are truly grateful to our mentor and guide at JGU, Prof. Dr. C. Raj Kumar, for his insightful contributions during the student Open-House and Constitution Museum sessions. His encouragement, honesty, and attentive listening were profound, making us feel more capable of re-imagining and an inch taller each time we left his office. We see in him a role model who embraces INTRApreneurship Dil-SE.

Additionally, we are truly grateful to the parents of Prof. Dr. Raj. Their encouragement, when we shared the possibility of bringing the world closer with 300 or more universities coming together, was truly affirming and reassuring. Having lost our father, the wise words from a compassionate man were so compelling that they profoundly motivated us to expedite this revolution.

Special thanks to our daughter, Khushi, whose joy and curiosity remind us daily of the importance of our work and the future we are striving to build. She ensures we maximize our gains from Raunakology and Khushiology each day, while being surrounded by our beloved pets, Bubbles and Cookie.
AND
A heartfelt appreciation to everyone at JGU who supported us in our journey to settle in Sonipat, both in big and small ways. Without their help, we wouldn't have experienced the true INTRApreneurial culture of JGU, which we believe is among the best universities for building **confidence, collaboration, and community**.

Malini & Ash Gulati | April 28, 2025 | Sonipat, India, Earth

# Earthizens ~ Song

From homizens to earthizens, we rise,
With hearts and minds, we realize,
A billion strong, we'll stand as one,
For Earth, our journey has begun.

GOLA, our goal, together we strive,
Homizens to earthizens, keeping hope alive,
In the Earthizens Revolution 2050, we find our way,
For a sustainable future, come what may.

With the Constitution of Earthizens, we'll guide,
Principles of unity, far and wide,
From homizens to earthizens, we'll transform,
For a planet where all can thrive and perform.

On Earthizens Day, October 31, we unite,
For the planet, we'll always fight,
With XYZ mindset, we'll achieve,
A world where all can truly breathe.

At the GOLA Conference, we'll share,
Ideas and dreams, beyond compare,
With universities, we'll pave the path,
To the future free from human's scath.

GOLA, our goal, together we strive,
Homizens to earthizens, keeping hope alive,
In the Earthizens Revolution 2050, we find our way,
For a sustainable future, come what may.

# Contents


Acknowledgment of Support ........................................................... 3

Earthizens ~ Song ....................................................................... 4

SECTION A ................................................................................ 8

Threat: Heaven Earth at Risk ......................................................... 8

   The Problem of Waste ............................................................. 8

   Air Pollution and Climate Change ............................................. 8

   The Threat of Asteroids, Aliens and New Viruses .......................... 8

   Fear of reduced population ..................................................... 9

SECTION B .............................................................................. 10

Solutions Re-Imagined !?! ........................................................... 10

   Sub-Section A: The S2S Path to Solution .................................. 10

   Sub-Section B: The Solution ................................................... 15

S2S Blueprint ~ Earthizens Revolution 2050 .................................. 17

SECTION C .............................................................................. 18

Solutions ~ Research Constructs ................................................. 18

Re-imagined: Lifetime ............................................................... 19

   Seeing EARTH with a different perspective ~ as a GOLA .............. 19

   Traveler To Heaven Earth ~ With 100 Years Extendable Visa ......... 20

   Estimated Year of Departure (EYD) .......................................... 21

   Happy Noon Day ................................................................. 21

Re-imagined: Earthizenship ........................................................ 23

   Homizens .......................................................................... 24

   Earthizens ......................................................................... 24

Re-imagined: Mindset ............................................................... 24

   XYZ Mindset: Spending with Purpose ...................................... 25

   XYZ preneurial Mindset: Earning with Purpose .......................... 25

   S2S | Pre-StartUPs | StartINs | Transformation Plans ................. 26

Re-imagined: Constitution .......................................................... 27

   Constitution for Homizens .................................................... 27

      FiT~ FaT Homes ......................................................... 29

      Homizens Academic Year ............................................. 29

   Constitution of Earthizens .................................................... 30

Earthizens of Eminence .................................................................30

Earthizens Day (Oct 31) ...............................................................30

SECTION D ...................................................................................34

Re-imagined: Role of Global Universities ...................................34

SECTION E ....................................................................................36

Exploring Re-imagined Mindset ..................................................36

Thought behind XYZ mindset ..................................................36

XYZ Consumer ......................................................................37

XYZ Producer .......................................................................38

XYZ Employee .......................................................................38

XYZ Investor .........................................................................38

XYZ Researcher ....................................................................38

XYZ Educator .......................................................................38

XYZ Adolescence ..................................................................39

XYZ Couples .........................................................................39

XYZ Eater .............................................................................40

XYZ Believer .........................................................................40

XYZ Sports ...........................................................................40

XYZ Govt...............................................................................41

XYZpreneurial Mindset ...........................................................41

The Challenge ......................................................................42

Re-imagining the Entrepreneurial Mindset...........................44

XYZ TAXONOMY for Sustainable Ventures ...........................44

XYZ Ashram Name ...............................................................47

SECTION F ....................................................................................50

Exploring Re-imagined Path to SDGs by AI .................................50

### Goal 1: No Poverty ............................................................52

### Goal 2: Zero Hunger .........................................................55

### Goal 3: Good Health and Well-being .................................58

### Goal 4: Quality Education ..................................................61

### Goal 5: Gender Equality .....................................................64

### Goal 6: Clean Water and Sanitation ..................................67

### Goal 7: Affordable and Clean Energy.................................70

*### Goal 8: Decent Work and Economic Growth* ...................73

*### Goal 9: Industry, Innovation, and Infrastructure* ...................76

*### Goal 10: Reduced Inequalities* ...................79

*### Goal 11: Sustainable Cities and Communities* ...................82

*### Goal 12: Responsible Consumption and Production* ...................86

*### Goal 13: Climate Action* ...................89

*### Goal 14: Life Below Water* ...................92

*### Goal 15: Life on Land* ...................95

*### Goal 16: Peace, Justice, and Strong Institutions* ...................98

*### Goal 17: Partnerships for the Goals* ...................101

SECTION G ...................106

Exploring Re-imagined FUTURE ...................106

Earthizens Revolution 2050 ...................106

Foundation Launch ...................106

Vision, Mission and Goals ...................107

Pilot Program (2028-2036) ...................108

Constitution of Earthizens ...................109

Universities Role: ...................109

Benefits to Universities: ...................110

Visibility and Recognition on WWW.CITIZEN.EARTH ...................110

Expanding our vision ...................111

Declared: Earthizens Revolution 2050 ...................112

References ...................113

APPENDICES ...................114

A : POLO Strategy for Sustainability ...................114

B : Glossary of Terms ...................117

C : Status check of words coined by author ...................120

About the Author ...................131

# SECTION A

# Threat: Heaven Earth at Risk

Earth is often referred to as a heaven, a paradise that we are fortunate to inhabit. This perspective is beautifully encapsulated in the words of astronaut Jim Lovell: **"You go to heaven when you are born."** Our planet provides everything we need to thrive—clean air, fresh water, fertile soil, and a diverse ecosystem. However, our current ways of living and creating are jeopardizing this paradise. The threats are many, but the opportunity lies in identifying those that matter most and prioritizing them. By doing so, we can prolong our journey and stay on this heavenly Earth, making it more welcoming for future generations.

## The Problem of Waste

One of the most pressing issues we face today is the generation of waste that the Earth cannot easily absorb. Our industrial processes, consumer habits, and lack of sustainable practices have led to an accumulation of waste that pollutes our land, water, and air. Plastics, electronic waste, and other non-biodegradable materials are filling our oceans and landfills, causing harm to wildlife and disrupting natural processes. By enrolling in the Earthizens Revolution 2050, universities can lead the charge in developing and promoting sustainable practices that reduce waste and encourage recycling and reuse.

## Air Pollution and Climate Change

Air pollution and climate change are two sides of the same coin, both resulting from our unsustainable practices. The burning of fossil fuels, deforestation, and industrial emissions have led to an increase in greenhouse gases, causing global temperatures to rise. This has resulted in more frequent and severe weather events, melting ice caps, rising sea levels, and disrupted ecosystems. The Earthizens Revolution 2050 aims to address these issues by promoting sustainable development goals (SDGs) that focus on reducing carbon emissions, transitioning to renewable energy sources, and protecting natural habitats.

## The Threat of Asteroids, Aliens and New Viruses

In addition to environmental challenges, we also face existential threats from asteroids and new viruses. While these may seem like distant possibilities, the reality is that we need to be prepared for such events. The COVID-19 pandemic has shown us how vulnerable we are to new viruses, and the potential impact of an asteroid collision could be catastrophic. Although the risk of nuclear warfare is also significant, it requires a different platform for discussion. The Earthizens Revolution 2050 includes plans to unite global efforts in developing strategies and technologies to detect and mitigate various threats.

## Fear of reduced population

A few decades ago, the fear of a declining population wasn't a common topic of discussion. However, with advancements in AI, data projections for the coming centuries have raised concerns among those who consider the broader implications. In the next 300 years, the global population is expected to be less than half of what it is today. The concern isn't about the reduced strain on resources, but rather the ongoing trend of decreasing birth rates per woman, decade after decade. This trend has significant implications for the roles humans play, especially as jobs are increasingly taken over by robots and drones. Are we witnessing the decline of our civilization, or is it that men, whose blue-collar jobs are mostly being taken over by robots, are going out of fashion? This is an interesting question that warrants further research.

While Jim thought, "**You go to heaven when you are born**," reflecting the beauty and abundance of Earth, this heaven is now under threat, and the disappointment is palpable. Our paradise is being tarnished by pollution, waste, and unsustainable practices. The air we breathe, the water we drink, and the soil that nourishes us are all at risk. The urgency to address these threats cannot be overstated; our collective efforts today will determine the fate of Earth for generations to come. We must confront these challenges with urgency and determination to restore and protect our home before it's too late. The time to act is now, and every moment counts.

# SECTION B

# Solutions Re-Imagined !?!

This section has two subsections. The first explains how the author arrived at this solution, and the second describes what the solution is. Let's first go through the sequence of events that led the author to this solution, while developing a completely new method for starting a venture, defined as S2S.

## Sub-Section A: The S2S Path to Solution

S2S is a technique proposed by the author to help individuals embrace solutions that may align with their life's purpose. This technique not only aids in problem-solving but also nurtures solutions like a parent, enabling them to become scalable. In practice, it's akin to SPFS, which stands for 'Solution – Purpose – Forenting – Scale'. The term "Forenting" is a newly coined word by the author, combining "Founder" and "Parenting" to express the passion founders have for nurturing their creations, knowing that one day these creations will operate independently, with many co-founders, role holders, and shareholders. Please note that this is still a fresh idea and requires extensive research.

The essence of S2S, or 'Solution to Scale,' lies in one's ability to re-imagine when the going gets tough. The author feels blessed to experience this culture of re-imagination on a large scale, from the architect to the gardener, faculty, administration, students, outreach, benefactors, and especially the Vice-Chancellor, at the intrapreneurial university JGU, where he is currently pursuing his PhD. He truly believes this approach has the potential to tackle the most complex challenges facing our planet.

This book is a tribute to the lessons learned in his life and at his universities, and an experiment in using the power of re-imagination to address the threats our Earth, The Gola, faces. Please note that this is a delicate trial by the author, with no intention to harm or demotivating anyone. Therefore, please read through the solution and the rest of the book in the spirit of a student eager to learn, rather than an expert providing research knowledge.

So, here below is the proposed solution, called Gola, Re-Imagined! This will be expressed in different parts to demonstrate the concept of S2S effectively.

PART 1:

It all started in March 2022, when the author relocated to join his wife to help build her career and take better care of her parents. They thought of sending a proposal to his wife's university for his employment. The logical option was to propose what the author was already doing in his previous employment at a university and express the domain where he felt he could help the new employer gain. The author was clear not to take up administration, for which the new university had given offers, but was interested in joining as a faculty member and towards innovation, which he was also involved in at his previous university.

The author wrote an email to his university, stating the possibility of joining as an Innovation Catalyst on March 22, 2022. As one of his expressions, he proposed the concept of  Earthizens of Eminence, which he saw as a unique solution for gaining attention from the university and building a global presence. The inspiration for the word "Eminence" came from the recognition that the government had decided to give to various universities, and the word "Earthizen" was coined by the author. He verified this by checking IPR websites and was happy to note that the keyword, which was part of a solution, was available, which he could call as his baby.

The solution visible to the author was in recognizing and awarding global individuals as 'Earthizens of Eminence' by the university to promote its cause and help our planet. He saw the purpose of life in this expression as it was larger, larger than the previous vision he had created with his wife for the Maths Revolution 2047, and scalable. Thus, they decided to parent the idea so that one day it becomes worthy of being a helping hand for humanity to make this heaven a better place for more. This was the completion of Part 1 of their story.

PART 2:

The second part of the story is in the parenting phase called pregnancy. Note that until late 2024, the idea and several others were emailed to the university, but the response was as silent as our gods provide. They only listen and do their part. That's what the author observed.

During the pregnancy phase, the purpose evolved to reimagine life on Earth as a blessing, as if given a chance to stay in some heaven, with oxygen, life, food, family, and everything that makes us alive. This helped create the concept of EYD and Noon Year, as explained later. The focus then shifted to reimagining life as a family at home, and how daily actions impact the way things get done on this planet, including production, consumption, waste, and the end of it all. These were the author's experiences as a house husband, which led to the XYZ mindset, emphasizing the importance of considering the end life of each product we touch or use.

This further led to seeing ourselves as homizens, akin to citizens of our homes, who must have rules and regulations to perform at our best. This concept was inspired by the author's learning at management schools, which taught the stages of forming, storming, norming, and performing. The author observed that storming often recurred due to poorly established norms, leading to delayed performance. Thus, the disciplined family concept called Homizens was born.

With Earthizens of Eminence already established, and while the university was preparing for the museum on the constitution of the country, the author further developed the name of the book that each household could build using AI. Initially thought of as The Book of Learning, which the author's family has been using for the last 15 years, it was reimagined as the Constitution of Homizens.

However, what each household does is driven by their city, religion, weather, profession, education, culture, etc., but much needs to be driven by what the Earth deserves and demands. Households may not be following this as required, and thus arose the need for a reference book called the Constitution of Earthizens. The author, along with Malini and another student at JGU, suggested writing a paper on this, which is still on the cards. As the author experienced the sessions on building the Constitution of India, his thoughts focused purely on the Constitution of Earthizens. While every session during the conference provided attendance to many, what the author took home were pearls of wisdom.

These thoughts defined the coming together of 300 universities, rather than individuals, as individuals may fade away and their third generation might not feel excited about something done decades ago. These live learnings also helped define the need for nine women to head this initiative, named Gola Foundation, along with their respective husbands. The author believes that the future will be more about women and robots managing, while men would also exist, although he doesn't have citations for this yet.

Once universities begin to show an inclusive direction year after year to at least a billion inhabitants of Earth, the planet is likely to benefit. However, two aspects remain unaddressed. Firstly, homizens represent one part of the spending side of money and resources, while companies, whose paramount goal is earning profits and providing greater value to shareholders, represent the other part. This aspect was unaddressed. Secondly, the timeline for this initiative remains unclear, as it is purely a re-imagination, while the actual implementation is necessary for success.

To resolve these issues and bring companies under the larger umbrella of Earthizens, the concept of XYZ mindset was extended to XYZpreneurial Mindset. Initially, there was an intention to write papers with university faculty, but despite numerous emails, meetings, and efforts between 2022 and 2024, the stars did not align. Consequently, the ideas were penned down as part of a larger book.

In the XYZpreneurial mindset, the significance of XYZ was re-imagined. The X factor represents the unique element, while the Y factor answers the question of 'why' something is being done, particularly if it benefits our heavenly Earth. The Y factor was linked to the Sustainable Development Goals (SDGs), providing a global standard for entrepreneurs to understand and relate to. Finally, there was a strong need to distinguish intrapreneurs and solopreneurs within the larger umbrella of entrepreneurship, which was achieved by placing them in the Z factor. With this, the XYZ framework was defined, and to address these questions, the concept of Ashram was introduced, offering a relatable answer. To understand these better the readers can explore further in later sections of this book.

PART 3:

Finally, to tie all this together so that libraries could have these captured in their books, one day, it was bundled as a revolution, with the name Earthizens Revolution 2050. This provided the timeline, that helped us visualize the pilot, its second phase and so on. It also established the urgency, pain, need and intention of work by addressing this as a revolution.

With all this done and documented the pre-startup phase of the S2S model stood complete. In this phase the author covered explained how they provided parenting to the purpose they found in the solution, while meandering to find opportunities to serve the university they found truly fascinating. The process is explained below in diagram form.

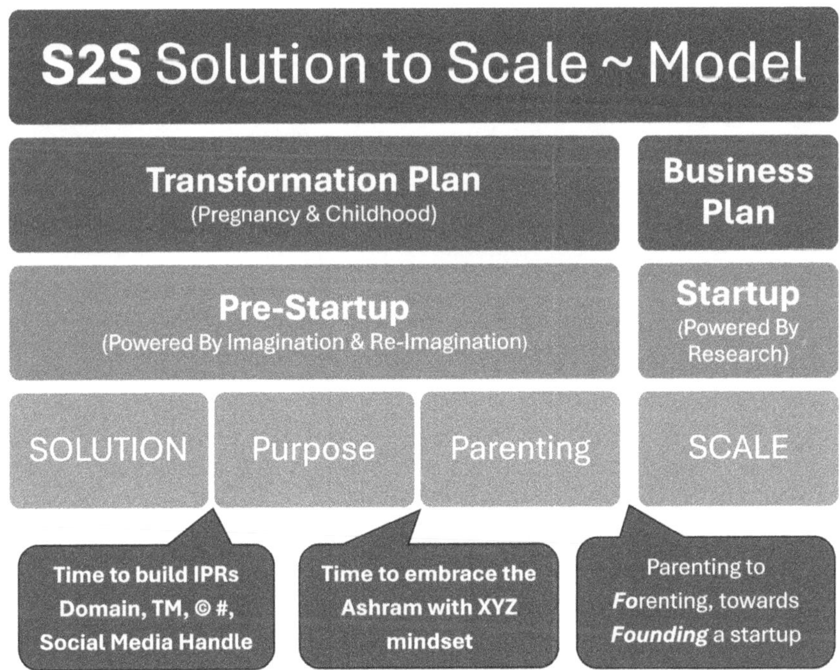


Diagram: **S2S** Solution to Scale is a construct open for academic study & research

To summarize, the journey began in March 2022 when the author relocated to support his wife's career and care for her parents. He proposed joining her university as an Innovation Catalyst, introducing the concept of "Earthizens of Eminence" to gain global attention and promote the university's cause. This idea aimed to recognize and award global individuals, fostering a larger purpose for humanity.

During the "pregnancy pre-startup phase," the author reimagined life on Earth as a blessing and developed concepts like EYD and Noon Year. He emphasized the importance of considering the end life of products and introduced the disciplined family concept of "Homizens." The need for a reference book, "Constitution of Earthizens," was identified to guide households in aligning their actions with Earth's needs.

The initiative was tied together under the "Earthizens Revolution 2050," establishing a timeline and urgency for the project. The pre-startup phase of the S2S multidisciplinary model was completed, documenting the author's journey and the development of the XYZpreneurial Mindset. This mindset redefined the significance of XYZ, linking it to Sustainable Development Goals and distinguishing intrapreneurs and solopreneurs within the larger umbrella of entrepreneurship.

All said and done, what's important is to build a better future for our dear Earth, a heaven for billions of us, of different species, as there is no other heaven like it to travel to. S2S with XYZpreneurial mindset is a new way discovered to save Earth, and GOLA!?! is an example in making.. and in case one still has doubts, please ask the Williams, who has just returned!

> The above example demonstrates how S2S was used to present the solution that came to the author, providing them with purpose in their imagination. With proper nurturing of the venture, including securing the IPRs, they were able to transition towards the parenting phase. But the step after parenting is scaling, which requires the formation of a company or induction into a company format. This movement involves the transfer of the venture from the parents to the foundation team, including the founders. This is a unique exit point for the parents and a fresh entry point for the team, to take it to its next phase of the S2S model.

> Further, with that, the pre-startup phase ends, and the startup phase begins. This transition is also when the transformation plan evolves into the business plan, and the venture moves out of a defined ashram, heading into a formal business phase, as shown in the S2S diagram.

> Similar solutions could inspire millions to find their purpose, excite them to provide parenting using law and the XYZ mindset, and prepare them with a company and business plan, only after defining the transformation plan and the ashram they belong to.

If you're being taught to create a business plan, remember that working on a transformation plan, understanding the ashram your venture belongs to, and preparing thoroughly before starting a company could help you de-stress and provide a smoother path to developing the essential business plan for your venture.

With that, let us try and embrace S2S and its benefits, discard what's not workable, and co-create something better on it, near it, or completely off it, just as we would with any impactful idea. This is especially crucial in an era where many faculty members, doctors, lawyers, and others are overwhelmed by the tsunami of AI. They can see the changes but struggle to comprehend what Bill is saying or what Khosla is shouting. It's time for us, the current & future faculty, teachers, school & university management, and UGCs of the world to read Dr. Spencer Johnson's 1998 book, Who Moved My Cheese?, because not only has the cheese moved, but so has the attention of our dear students.

## Sub-Section B: The Solution

Welcome to "GOLA, Re-imagined !?!", a visionary blueprint designed to unite the strategy teams of 300 global universities in a collective effort to lead the Earthizens Revolution 2050. The title "GOLA, Re-imagined !?!" is intentionally punctuated with '!?!' to reflect a blend of assertion, doubt, and inquiry. This punctuation signifies that while the re-imagination is slated with confidence, it also acknowledges the uncertainties and challenges ahead, posing a question to the global community to join in this collective endeavor.

> Inspired by the concept of GOLA, a term popularized by Hindi movies referring to our beloved Earth, this book aims to chart a path towards a sustainable future. Homizens and Earthizens—conscious global citizens— will work together to achieve the 17 Sustainable Development Goals (SDGs) with a re-imagined spirit of Earthizenship as the key idea.

To justify the reader's time investment, the author has ensured that this book is not just a call to action but a comprehensive guide outlining the blueprint, re-imagined concepts, and the steps to be taken in the near future to achieve this ambitious goal. It is expected to serve as a roadmap for 300 global universities, who could be the founding members of the Constituent Assembly for the Constitution of Earthizens by 2028-36, laying the foundation for Earthizens Revolution 2050.

The author believes that the sustainability opportunity from 2025 to 2050 is immense and multifaceted. To harness this potential, platforms adopting the concept of S2S – Solutions 2 Scale are needed. This approach focuses on education and skill-building to scale solutions to global problems. The key idea of S2S is: *Once a solution addressing any of the SDGs is conceived, humanity must work collectively to test its validity and ensure it is accessible to all.*

A well-structured S2S model named Earthizens Revolution 2050 has been visualized by the author for this revolution. It needs rigorous testing, refining, and scaling the solution to meet diverse needs across different regions. By making these solutions universally accessible, global challenges can be effectively tackled, and sustainability goals achieved. With that, entrepreneurs are invited with enthusiasm to join this global effort, embracing an XYZpreneurial mindset to safeguard Earth.

To build more of such S2S models with XYZpreneurial mindsets, the author invites a fresh new re-imagination of the global society as a single large body, with each institution playing its valid vital role. This role is critical to ensure that each homizen works towards being an Earthizen, in the spirit of Earthizenship, while respecting the established institutions as much they desire.

Understanding that the proposed global universities would play a significant role, this proposal put forward a researchable construct of imagining these universities as the lungs of the large body of proposed Earthizens, embodying the spirit of Earthizenship. Meanwhile, other important entities could represent other vital parts of this large body, as outlined below:

**Religion (The Heart):** The heart's chambers symbolize various religions, working in harmony to pump life-giving blood throughout the body. Different religions can coexist to foster compassion, empathy, and a sense of community, creating a more unified and understanding world with 8 billion of us co-existing. This visualization emphasizes inclusivity and interdependence while highlighting the distinct characteristics that set them apart.

**Countries (The Brain):** The brain's hemispheres represent different political ideologies. One symbolizes capitalist ideals, the other socialist principles. Both are essential for balanced thinking and decision-making. Similarly, countries with diverse political systems can collaborate to address global challenges, combining their strengths to create a more inclusive and cooperative world. This visualization ensures that most types of economies are represented.

**Corporations (The Digestive System):** The stomach and intestines represent the economic engine of society. Large corporations are symbolized by the large intestine, while small businesses are represented by the small intestine. Both are crucial for economic growth and innovation. By aligning their goals with social and environmental objectives, corporations can contribute to a more equitable and sustainable future. This visualization highlights the diversity of economic units that help families earn their energy, food, and income.

The author believes this vision can be realized if each household follows its own religion within its own country, working for different types of organizations, while adhering to simple, pro-Earth rules as Earthizens would. This would be guided by the Constitution of Earthizens, which the 300 universities, the lungs of our Gola, would build, monitor, realign, and maintain for the common good.

With that, the S2S Blueprint of this revolution, provided below, needs to be explored further in the book to understand the detailed proposal for this transformation plan.

## S2S Blueprint ~ Earthizens Revolution 2050

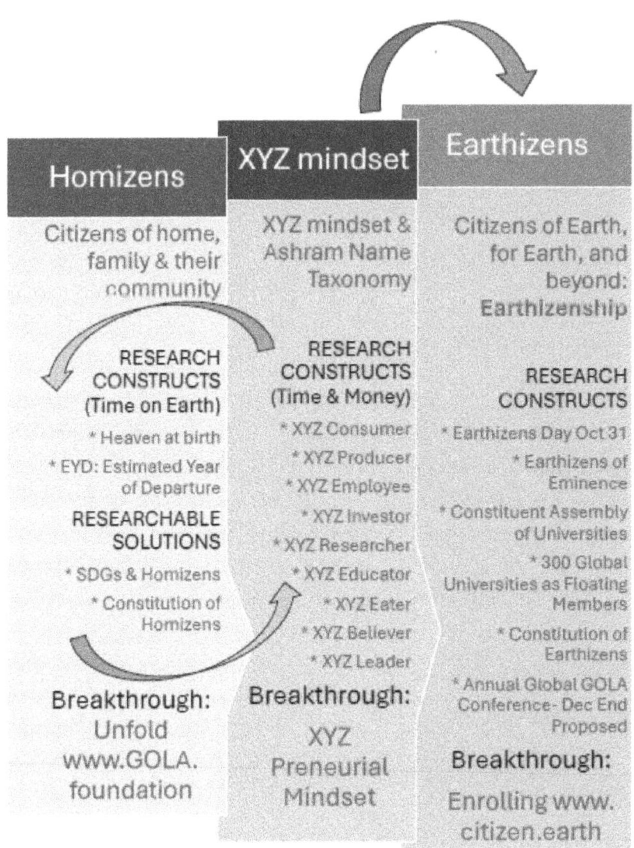

# SECTION C

# Solutions ~ Research Constructs

In today's rapidly evolving world, the concept of reimagination requires attention.

Traditional approaches to problem-solving and innovation are no longer sufficient to address the complex and interconnected challenges we face. While offering reimagined solutions to future generations, it is our responsibility to ensure that these offerings are thoroughly researched, vetted, and tested. This ensures that the best of our reimagined ideas are presented, yielding the highest results at the lowest cost. We propose the following constructs for rigorous research to help us better embrace our planet.

Reimagination, as I am learning as a university student, stands for breaking free from conventional thinking and embracing a holistic, forward-thinking mindset. It involves integrating diverse perspectives, harnessing cutting-edge technologies, and fostering a culture of continuous learning and adaptation. This approach encourages us to envision bold, sustainable solutions that not only mitigate current issues but also anticipate future challenges.

For instance, urban planning must evolve to create resilient, green cities that prioritize both human well-being and ecological balance, rather than focusing solely on concepts like density and reduced pollution. Renewable energy sources need to be scaled up and integrated into every aspect of our lives, not just to reduce our reliance on fossil fuels, but also to ensure that these options do not become a burden on the Earth at their end-of-life. Additionally, we must rethink our consumption patterns, promoting circular economies that minimize waste and maximize resource efficiency, rather than emphasizing how to sell more in universities across the globe.

By embracing reimagination, we can cultivate a more sustainable and equitable future, and I sincerely agree. This paradigm shift is essential to preserving our planet for future generations, ensuring that we not only survive but thrive in harmony with the Earth for the next hundreds of years.

As a PhD student at my university, at age 51, I wholeheartedly support the concept of reimagination. This tribute to reimagination reflects my commitment to exploring and rethinking many of the aspects mentioned below, even at the risk of being ridiculed or considered too imaginative. With that, here are a few humble thoughts, offered with fear, hesitation, and doubts, as they are so fresh that even Google doesn't recognize more than a few as valid words. Let's reimagine...

# Re-imagined: Lifetime

In this reimagination, we embark on a transformative journey that challenges our conventional perceptions of existence on this planet. By adopting the perspective of an astronaut, we see Earth not as an immense expanse but as a small, precious "GOLA" in the vast cosmos. This shift in viewpoint fosters a profound appreciation for our home, highlighting its unique value and the unparalleled freedom it offers. As we explore the concept of Earth as a heaven with a 100-year extendable visa, we are reminded of the fleeting nature of our time here and the responsibility we bear to cherish and enhance this sanctuary.

This re-imagination draws inspiration from astronaut Jim Lovell's words, "You go to heaven when you are born," transforming our existence into a journey of discovery, growth, and contribution. We are visitors in this magnificent realm, entrusted with the duty to preserve and improve it for ourselves and future generations. By embracing this mindset, we cultivate a sense of belonging and purpose, knowing that our actions contribute to the collective well-being. Additionally, the concept of "Happy Noon Day" encourages us to celebrate our age by reflecting on the milestones we achieve, particularly upon reaching 50 years, fostering hope and new possibilities.

## Seeing EARTH with a different perspective ~ as a GOLA

While being on Earth, we perceive our surroundings as vast and overwhelming, a notion reinforced by mathematics and our sense of judgment. However, this perspective shifts dramatically when we venture beyond our atmosphere. Observing Earth from space, we see it as a smaller "GOLA" (spherical object), dwarfed by other planets, stars, and galaxies. From an astronaut's viewpoint, Earth stands out as the only place where we experience unparalleled freedom, despite its limitations. This realization deepens our appreciation for Earth as our home, a unique sanctuary in the vast cosmos. It brings a profound sense of connection and responsibility towards our planet, emphasizing its irreplaceable value.

We believe that experiencing Earth as immense from the perspective of a bystander on its surface is valid. Yet, from the vantage point of an astronaut, Earth may appear as a small "GOLA." Both perspectives hold truth. Through this book, we invite readers to adopt the astronaut's viewpoint, gaining a deeper understanding and appreciation of our planet's unique place in the universe.

## Traveler To Heaven Earth ~ With 100 Years Extendable Visa

"Congratulations! You've been granted a visa for 100 years or more to Earth, the heaven bestowed upon the 8 billion lucky ones so far. However, with the deteriorating conditions of this heaven, in the next 300 years, visas are likely to be reduced by half. Therefore, live life to the fullest and make the most of this opportunity while ensuring that you do your best to make it a better heaven for future visitors. These efforts may set you apart for additional visits to future heavens, defined solely by your deeds," as Earth said.

As expressed earlier, this reimagination draws inspiration from the perspective beautifully encapsulated in the words of astronaut Jim Lovell: **'You go to heaven when you are born.'** This viewpoint transforms our existence into a journey of discovery, growth, and contribution on this heaven. We are visitors in this magnificent realm, entrusted with the responsibility to cherish and enhance it for ourselves, our peers, and future generations, forming a compelling belief.

Thereby, in this heaven, every moment becomes an opportunity to appreciate the beauty around us. The vibrant colors of nature, the symphony of birds, and the gentle rustle of leaves in the wind remind us of the paradise we inhabit. Our interactions with others are imbued with kindness and empathy, fostering a community where love and respect flourish. By embracing this XYZ mindset, as explained later, we cultivate a sense of belonging and purpose, knowing that our actions contribute to the collective well-being.

As visitors with a limited visa, we are motivated to make the most of our time. We strive to leave a positive impact, whether through small acts of kindness or grand gestures of innovation. Our efforts to improve the environment, support social causes, and promote peace become the legacy we leave behind. This heaven is not just a place to live but a canvas for our dreams and aspirations.

Moreover, this perspective encourages us to think beyond our individual lives. We recognize the importance of sustainability and the need to preserve this heaven for future generations. Our choices reflect a commitment to creating a better world, where the next visitors can experience the same, if not greater, beauty and harmony.

In essence, viewing Earth as our first heaven that we recollect visiting, with a 100-year visa, inspires us to live with intention and gratitude. It reminds us that we are part of something greater, a cosmic journey that continues beyond our time here. By making this heaven better, we open the door to the possibility of another, even more wondrous heaven somewhere in the universe.

## Estimated Year of Departure (EYD)

Inspired by the imagination above, we move to our second re-imagined research construct. Recognizing that our time on Earth is finite, it becomes crucial to view our lives through various lenses to ensure we live meaningfully and sustainably. Estimating an end to this journey while living each moment can heighten our awareness each day, month, and year. Otherwise, time keeps flying, and the end reaches us much before we live fully. Therefore, the concept of EYD (Estimated Year of Departure) encourages us to reflect on our journey and embrace the years that follow with purpose and grace.

This vision suggests that our imaginary visa for this journey on Earth could be considered valid for around 100 years (or as much or less as one may like) and can be extended beyond, motivating us to make the most of the years we have. Note that this is a research construct and thus requires proper research to be expressed with greater confidence. Considering that 100 years equate to approximately 36,500 days, we can view our time here as having a biological battery life of these days. If we maintain, change, and take care of this biological battery well, assuming accidents and other unforeseen events do not damage it, we can maximize our time on Earth.

By not proposing a fixed rule for calculating EYD, individuals are encouraged to embrace the freedom to set their own estimates. This allows them to express themselves or refrain without feeling burdened or stressed, thereby maintaining a sense of personal freedom.

## Happy Noon Day

Another aspect is the celebration of the age we achieve. We recommend expressing our age by the Birth Noon instead of the Birthday upon reaching 50 years. Thus, the 50th Birthday could be celebrated as Birth Noon Day or just as the Noon Day, rather than a Birthday. This approach encourages reflection on the "Half Plus Age" and the enjoyment of those refreshing, youthful years beyond 50. This celebration could help build hope, create new possibilities and realizations, build ability to re-imagine and restart.

For example, at age 55, Malini and I will be HALF plus 5, while our self-chosen EYD being the year 2050, as our estimate of the time we may depart, provided all goes well till then. Statistically, there is a strong chance that we may depart earlier, but by expressing this, we become truly aware of the limited time we have to give back to our Earth for gracing us with this opportunity of life. No wonder both the Maths Revolution and the Earthizens Revolution we have proposed max out by the year 2050, as we truly wish to give back in ways more than many. Before we build more, let's share the song for 50th birthday celebrations.

🎵 Happy Noon Day Song 🎵

Happy Noon Day to you,
A milestone to pursue,
Halfway through our journey,
With dreams still shining through.

Happy Noon Day, to you,
For the joy that life brings to you,
Half plus age, we celebrate,
With hearts so full, as it's never too late.

At fifty, we reflect,
On the moments we collect,
Grateful for the years we've had,
And the future, bright and glad.

Every year a chance to give,
To our Earth, where we live,
Changing habits, forming new,
Extending life, it's up to you.

Happy Noon Day, to you,
For the joy that life brings to you,
Half plus age, we celebrate,
With hearts so full, as it is never too late.

The key idea is to not take life for granted and to recognize that the average human lifespan on this planet may be around 100 years, more or less. This is an honest expression that many may find uncomfortable, but it's important to acknowledge that time is flying and slipping out of our hands. Why not celebrate what we have left, especially after age 50? Let us embrace the Happy Noon Day Song for turning 50, 'Our half century,' as our friend Aziz would have said.

We believe this declaration could help us view each passing year as a diminishing opportunity to give back to our planet. Conversely, it could inspire us to take critical actions to improve our chances of extending the Estimated Years of Life (EYD), which might involve changing old habits and forming new, beneficial ones.

By embracing these principles, we can work towards departing from Earth gracefully, aiming to leave a positive and lasting impact. This journey from Homizen to Earthizen is a commitment to living in harmony with the planet, ensuring a better future for all.

## Re-imagined: Earthizenship

Earthizenship is a new term coined by Ash Gulati, the author of this book, to express the roles, duties, and responsibilities we all have as natural inhabitants of Earth. While we are divided by well-defined and justified borders that require formal citizenship of a specific country according to global rules and regulations, Earthizenship offers a different perspective.

To clarify, citizens of all countries can be considered eligible for Earthizenship, but not all those eligible for Earthizenship can be granted citizenship of a country of their choice.

Earthizenship is more of a symbolic expression and not a legal statement yet, reminding us that while we may divide ourselves by land and earn different citizenships, we cannot separate ourselves from the air we breathe, the weather we face, the rains we get, the Earth's rotation that defines day and night, the sun's heat that creates clouds and rain, or the Earth's gravity that keeps oceanic water from falling off the planet. Observe that we can celebrate the moon in different ways, but we cannot divide or own the gravity it provides, which causes oceanic waves each night in those massive seas.

Furthermore, Earthizenship is not a religion called Earthism, nor are Earthists followers of such a religion. We believe our existing religions are precious and provide hope to their followers. Personally, I believe in all religions and consider myself an Omnist.

On the flip side, Earthizenship could strongly be about being earthy, earthier, or earthiest, which describe someone as open and direct, discussing subjects others might avoid or feel hesitant about. If you describe something as earthy, you mean it looks, smells, or feels like earth. Being earthy could now ideally be expressed as someone who truly embraces the opportunity of being on this earth, without the fear of not being here someday, and connects with its different facets with happiness, inclusivity, and togetherness while alive on this planet. How would that be?

With all that above, Earthizenship is re-imagined through the concepts of "Homizens" and "Earthizens," emphasizing the role of individuals and households in driving global change. Let us now understand their relationship and how they complement each other.

Homizens are citizens of homes who take responsibility for their actions, understanding their choices impact the planet. Raised in environments that prioritize responsibility, empathy, and eco-friendly practices, these Homizens evolve into Earthizens—advocates for global sustainability.

This transformation symbolizes a shift in consciousness and responsibility. As Earthizens, they champion sustainable practices and contribute to the Sustainable Development Goals (SDGs), inspiring others to follow their path. Thus, Earthizenship is re-imagined as a journey from personal responsibility to global advocacy. Let us try and understand each in a better way and in greater detail.

## Homizens

The term "Homizens," coined by the author of this book, directly addresses the citizens of homes, emphasizing the importance of individual and household actions in driving global change. By focusing on "Homizens," the revolution highlights the need for each person to take responsibility for their choices and actions, recognizing that how we earn and spend impacts the planet in significant ways. This grassroots approach ensures that the movement starts from the ground up, making it more inclusive and impactful.

According to the author, Homizens can be seen as the offspring of sustainable parenting. Raised in environments that prioritize responsibility, empathy, and eco-friendly practices, they develop the ability to care for both their homes and the broader world. This nurturing process eventually transforms them into Earthizens, who advocate for global sustainability.

## Earthizens

The journey from Homizens to Earthizens represents a significant transformation. As individuals and households adopt sustainable practices and contribute to the SDGs, they are honored by being addressed as Earthizens. This recognition not only celebrates their efforts but also motivates others to follow suit. The transition from Homizens to Earthizens symbolizes the achievement of a higher level of consciousness and responsibility towards the planet. Let us explore this in greater detail in the sections ahead of this book.

# Re-imagined: Mindset

The Earthizens Revolution 2050 introduces the XYZ Mindset, which emphasizes mindful spending and earning with purpose. It encourages Homizens to support genuinely sustainable products and companies, driving market changes towards more ethical practices. The revolution also promotes the XYZpreneurial mindset, urging individuals to align their business practices with the Sustainable Development Goals (SDGs). This proactive approach includes focusing on Pre-Startups, StartINs, and early transformation planning, ensuring that businesses are sustainable and impactful from the outset. By fostering these mindsets, the revolution aims to accelerate progress towards a more sustainable and ethical future. Let us learn more about them.

## XYZ Mindset: Spending with Purpose

The revolution emphasizes the importance of mindful spending, not just saving. Homizens are encouraged to support products and companies that genuinely respect the SDGs, rather than those that engage in greenwashing or superficial sustainability efforts. This shift in consumer behavior can drive significant changes in the market, as businesses are incentivized to adopt more sustainable practices to meet the demands of conscious consumers. This concept is further elaborated as the XYZ mindset, with greater details.

## XYZ preneurial Mindset: Earning with Purpose

A cornerstone of the Earthizens Revolution 2050 is the encouragement for individuals to make conscious choices in their earning methods. Whether as solopreneurs, intrapreneurs, or entrepreneurs, Homizens are urged to align their business practices with the Sustainable Development Goals (SDGs).

This approach involves creating value in ways that are sustainable, ethical, and beneficial to the planet. By promoting this mindset, the revolution accelerates progress towards the SDGs, as more businesses adopt practices that contribute to environmental and social well-being. This is addressed further as XYZpreneurial mindset, and Ashram taxonomy with greater details.

This is critical, especially for a country like India and those that admire our way of life, democracy, and constitution. Unlike capitalist economies such as the USA, where money for setting up businesses flows comfortably, or countries like China, where the government is highly structured, dominant, and disciplined, India faces unique challenges. The ecosystem here is less developed, leading to many ventures started by citizens failing and causing significant pain, which may not be the case in the USA or China.

In India, money often comes from selling parents' or wife's jewelry, putting the house as collateral with a bank, or borrowing from family and friends using post-dated cheques and other methods. In case of failure, the pain is much greater. This calls for a mindset that goes beyond the traditional rewards of entrepreneurship, such as money and fame. We need to build intrinsic motivation to solve problems in the same land and environment where these young entrepreneurs live, breathe, have relationships, win, lose, and still survive with dignity.

An XYZpreneurial mindset could provide more options anchored on 'purpose' after failure for these young souls, who may face the end of their passion, venture, or, in the worst case, their own energy. This represents a national loss, and we must re-imagine and present better alternatives not just for our country but also for the 100-plus nations that truly admire us.

## S2S | Pre-StartUPs | StartINs | Transformation Plans

The XYZpreneurial mindset is characterized by a strong focus on the concept of S2S – Solutions 2 Scale. This approach incorporates Pre-Startups, StartINs, and the development of a transformation plan well before working on a detailed business plan. By emphasizing these elements, the XYZpreneurial mindset ensures that entrepreneurs are prepared to scale their solutions effectively while experiencing 'purpose' and 'parenting' before achieving success, which aligns with the Sustainable Development Goals (SDGs).

Pre-Startups involve identifying and nurturing potential business ideas before they officially become startups. This phase is crucial for validating concepts, understanding market needs, and building a solid foundation without actually starting the company or organization. By focusing on Pre-Startups, entrepreneurs can ensure that their ideas are well-grounded and have a higher chance of success.

StartINs refer to the pre-startup phase of intrapreneurial ideas within an organization. These are innovative concepts developed by employees that have the potential to transform the business from within. By fostering StartINs, organizations can leverage internal talent and creativity to drive growth and innovation, making the business more dynamic and adaptable.

Moreover, the XYZpreneurial mindset prioritizes developing a transformation plan well before crafting a detailed business plan. This approach ensures that entrepreneurs have a clear vision of the changes and impacts their business will bring to the market and society. By focusing on transformation first, entrepreneurs can align their strategies with long-term goals and societal needs, making their ventures more sustainable and impactful. This forward-thinking approach not only enhances the chances of success but also fosters a culture of continuous improvement and adaptability, which are essential in today's dynamic business environment.

The sustainability opportunity from 2025 to 2050 is immense and multifaceted. To harness this potential, we need to create platforms that adopt the concept of S2S. This approach focuses on education and skill-building aimed at scaling solutions once ideated to address global problems. Once a solution addressing any of the SDGs is conceived, humanity must work collectively to test its validity and ensure it is accessible to all. This involves rigorous testing, refining, and scaling the solution to meet diverse needs across different regions.

By making these solutions universally accessible, we can effectively tackle global challenges and achieve our sustainability goals. This collaborative effort will not only validate the solutions but also empower communities worldwide, fostering a sustainable future for all. The XYZpreneurial mindset, with its emphasis on Pre-Startups, StartINs, and early transformation planning, provides a robust framework for achieving these goals and driving meaningful change.

# Re-imagined: Constitution

The constitution as a document stands re-imagined here. This comes from the success we have seen of these documents to run big, diverse economies like that of India. Taking a clue from having a structured document our reimagination takes us to something similar that each home has, which eventually aligns with the one we all get made for our planet Earth.

The Earthizens Revolution 2050 introduces personalized constitutions for Homizens, powered by AI, to align individual and family goals with the Sustainable Development Goals (SDGs). These constitutions offer tailored guidelines, fostering a harmonious and supportive environment through mutually accepted rules. The revolution emphasizes the importance of small and big actions in defining the fitness of homes, promoting sustainable practices. Homes are categorized as fit or fat based on their sustainability practices, with fit homes utilizing resources efficiently and fat homes characterized by wastage.

The GOLA Foundation supports this initiative by providing digital tools for annual performance evaluation, helping families progress through stages of Homizenship: Copper, Bronze, Silver, Gold, and Platinum. This journey, culminating in Earthizenship, empowers families to contribute significantly to global sustainability and well-being. Exceptional families may be recognized as Earthizens of Eminence, celebrating their outstanding contributions during the annual conference. Together, we can create a world where every Homizen thrives and contributes to the collective well-being of our planet.

## Constitution for Homizens

The proposed Earthizens Revolution 2050 introduces the innovative concept of personalized constitutions for Homizens, powered by AI. These constitutions provide tailored guidelines to help individuals and families align their goals with those of Earthizens, derived from the SDGs. This personalized approach ensures that each person receives relevant and actionable advice, making it easier for them to contribute to the global mission. By leveraging AI, the revolution can provide scalable and effective support to millions of Homizens worldwide. This base document could have some mutually accepted rules by the family that they all agree to follow.

Examples of some key elements of a sample Constitution of Homizens could include agreements on certain norms that make interactions within the family, its new members, and others associated with them easier. These norms or rules might include asking for permission before using someone else's belongings, sharing one positive thing that happened each day, allowing each family member private time when needed without questions, being punctual for family activities or meals, communicating plans or schedule changes in advance, adhering to curfews or agreed plans to build trust, celebrating small achievements together and not just major events, celebrating each person's individuality without judgment or comparison, and keeping phones away during meals to encourage conversation.

Additionally, working together to solve family issues instead of blaming, honoring commitments to the family like attending planned events, speaking calmly to each other even when disagreeing, taking turns choosing what to watch or play during family time, speaking kindly about family members even when they're not present, keeping shared spaces tidy as everyone's responsibility, starting and ending each day by greeting each other warmly, respecting everyone's need for quiet or alone time, avoiding interrupting when someone else is speaking, and dividing household tasks fairly according to age and capability are important norms.

Furthermore, apologizing when you've hurt someone regardless of your intentions, offering help with tasks without waiting to be asked, always saying goodbye and checking in when leaving the house, addressing issues calmly instead of holding grudges, providing constructive feedback rather than criticism, staying calm and supportive during emergencies or stressful moments, showing gratitude when someone does something for you, regularly showing affection through words, gestures, or actions, holding weekly family meetings to discuss issues and plans, cleaning up any mess you make right away, and sharing pet care responsibilities equally are essential practices. These norms and rules help create a harmonious and supportive family environment.

As we shall evolve we would reach a point where all individuals shall have their own constitution as Selfizens, aligned with their homes, their religion, country, culture, organization they work for, groups they believe in, and eventually aligning with the constitution of Earthizens, for the true spirit of Earthizenship.

## FiT~ FaT Homes

These small and big things eventually define how fit we are as Homizens. Further norms, as suggested with specific SDGs later in the book, provide insights into how "fat" our homes could be. The more wastage there is, the more purchases are made, and the less we give up, the fatter the home could be considered. Conversely, the better we utilize the emotions and nonphysical aspects of being in a home, the more well-kept and fit our home will be. These are critical aspects that define the hygiene, growth, and health of the family in more ways than one. A set of rules, with the structure and spirit of a constitution, could help resolve many small issues that arise as the home team is either formed or growing. The principles of forming, storming, norming, and performing work well in this context.

Accordingly, the Constitution of Homizens shall be managed collaboratively by the family, ensuring that each member adheres to the mutually accepted rules and guidelines. This collective effort fosters a harmonious environment for supportive decision making, where everyone contributes to the shared goals.

## Homizens Academic Year

The GOI A Foundation will play a crucial role by providing advanced digital tools to evaluate performance annually (Sep 01 to Aug 31 ~ Homizens Academic Year), enabling families to track their progress and move from Copper Homizens to Bronze, Silver, Gold, and ultimately Platinum status. These tools will facilitate the sharing of evaluation videos and peer-reviewed proof, ensuring transparency and accountability. This process will meet the stringent criteria that will evolve through the constituent assembly of up to 300 Universities, which shall take charge of the academic standards, during the Pilot Phase 2028-36.

As families advance through these stages, they will not only enhance their own well-being but also contribute significantly to the global mission of Earthizens. This progression from Homizens to higher levels of Homizenship, and eventually to Earthizenship, is celebrated annually on October 31, Earthizens Day. Exceptional families may be recognized as Earthizens of Eminence for their outstanding contributions, and they are awarded and celebrated during the annual conference held globally before Christmas each year.

This journey, powered by AI and supported by the GOLA Foundation, will empower families to achieve their full potential, aligning their personal goals with the Sustainable Development Goals (SDGs) and fostering a brighter future for all. Together, we can create a world where every Homizen thrives, contributing to the collective well-being of our planet while advancing in status to become Earthizens.

## Constitution of Earthizens

The Earthizens Revolution 2050 also prepares individuals and communities to unite against global threats such as asteroids and new viruses. By fostering a sense of global Earthizenship and cooperation, the revolution ensures we are better equipped to face these challenges, in addition to the needs specified above. The creation of the Constitution of Earthizens provides a framework for coordinated action, ensuring our collective efforts are aligned and effective. This construct requires significant work by universities, necessitating the involvement of 300 institutions to ensure inclusiveness. The constitution is designed to be dynamic, continuously upgraded and present everywhere, without a single targeted owner.

### Earthizens of Eminence

This initiative recognizes individuals who have made significant contributions to environmental conservation and sustainability. These "earthizens" serve as role models, inspiring others to join the movement. By highlighting their achievements, the revolution aims to motivate more people to act and make a difference in their communities. Our goal is to recognize 1% of the global population as role models by the year 2050, so that humanity can understand, accept, and work towards the betterment of our planet. By following those in their own community, city, and country who have made a mark according to global standards, we can foster widespread change.

To ensure that these global standards are well-vetted and robust, they will be audited at various levels with increasing objectivity and decreasing subjectivity. The responsibility to define, polish, audit, and reimagine these norms until they are closest to perfection will lie with the 300 universities that come together to support this initiative.

### Earthizens Day (Oct 31)

Celebrated on October 31st, Earthizens Unity Day is a global event that unites people in their commitment to the planet. It serves as a reminder of our collective responsibility and the progress we have made towards sustainability. On this day, various activities and events are organized worldwide to raise awareness about environmental issues and celebrate the achievements of the Earthizens Revolution, which is projected to be at its peak by the year 2050.

Coinciding with Earthizens Day, World Cities Day (UN) and National Unity Day in India are celebrated by billions of people of diverse castes, religions, and states. The word "citizen" originates from "cities," which the UN celebrates, and "unity" is celebrated as National Unity Day by Indians, including us. Each year, on October 31st, these celebrations bring humans across the globe together with great pride and honor to commemorate their citizenship in some form. This dual celebration, already established as a norm, highlights the interconnectedness of global and national efforts towards a more sustainable and harmonious world.

Therefore, it was resolved to celebrate Earthizens Unity Day on October 31st each year. In addition to the personal regard for this date, this specific date was chosen to emphasize the unity and shared responsibility we are already celebrating towards our planet. By aligning Earthizens Unity Day with World Cities Day and National Unity Day, we reinforce the importance of global and national collaboration in achieving sustainability. This celebration serves as a powerful reminder that our efforts are interconnected and that together, we can make significant strides towards a better future for all Earthizens.

Here are the well-considered, logical, and widely accepted reasons that were thoroughly discussed to finalize celebrating Earthizens Day on October 31, distinct from Earth Day, which is observed annually on April 22:

**Human-Centric Focus:** Earthizens Day emphasizes human actions and behaviors that are friendlier to Earth, distinguishing it from Earth Day, which celebrates the planet itself and its natural processes overall.

**Recognition of Progress:** Earthizens Day celebrates the journey of individuals and families as they progress through various levels of Homizens (Copper, Bronze, Silver, Gold, Platinum) to become Earthizens and Earthizens of Eminence, emphasizing sustainable living practices. In contrast, Earth Day focuses more on expressing gratitude to the planet, with less emphasis on connecting families as units under the Earth as an umbrella entity.

**Celebrating Achievements:** Earthizens Day is akin to celebrating the achievements of responsible and conscientious individuals, reflecting the spirit of good parenting. Earth Day, on the other hand, is more like celebrating the birthday of Earth.

**Celebrating Unity and Urban Progress:** The decision to celebrate Earthizens Day on October 31st is based on more than many well-founded, known, inviting and already established reasons. Two of the most significant ones are expressed below.

Firstly, it aligns with World Cities Day, established by United Nations General Assembly resolution and celebrated annually on October 31st. This date symbolizes organization, discipline, and structure, reflecting the essence of urban living. Interestingly, the word "citizen" is derived from the word "city," highlighting the deep connection between urban centers and the people who inhabit them, as we know.

Additionally, National Unity Day, or Rashtriya Ekta Diwas, is observed in India on October 31st to honor the birth anniversary of Sardar Vallabhbhai Patel. This day promotes national integration, unity, and harmony among citizens, recognizing Patel's pivotal role in uniting the princely states into the Indian Union after independence.

Together, these celebrations foster a spirit of giving back, harmony, unity, and togetherness, embodying the essence of our re-imagined future. Earthizens Day on October 31st each year not only commemorates these significant events but also encourages us to reflect on our shared responsibilities and the importance of working together to build a better world for all.

**Humans Need Discipline**: While Earth Day celebrates all life forms on our planet, Earthizens Day is dedicated to encouraging humans to be more disciplined, conscious, and responsible in their relationship with Earth.

It's crucial to recognize that although humans make up less than say 5% of the total biomass on Earth, we control, manage, extract, and utilize resources as if there is not much regard for the other biomass that coexists with us. This imbalance highlights the urgent need for Earthizens Day, a day dedicated to fostering a more respectful and sustainable relationship between humans and our planet. It is our responsibility to behave like good earthizens of our own Earth.

**Educational Awards:** Earthizens Day includes the global recognition of eminent Earthizens by universities & schools, known as 'Earthizens of Eminence'. This initiative promotes role models as a tool for better environmental stewardship, highlighting the significant role that universities and schools play in this effort.

**Legal and International Affairs:** Earthizenship falls under the domain of law and international affairs, whereas Earth Day is more aligned with environmental and biosciences.

**Future Endeavors:** The future of Earthizenship is shaped by global universities, particularly those focusing on law and international affairs. In contrast, Earth Day involves broader societal and scientific efforts, including contributions from NGOs, governments, and companies.

**Distinct Celebrations:** Having separate dates ensures that both Earth Day and Earthizens Day receive focused attention and resources, maximizing their individual impacts.

**Extended Awareness:** Celebrating Earthizens Day on October 31st extends the period of environmental awareness and action beyond Earth Day, sustaining momentum and engagement throughout the year. This ensures there are two events each year, with a gap of almost 6 months, helping momentum.

These reasons collectively support the idea of having a distinct date for Earthizens Day, ensuring that both celebrations can effectively achieve their unique goals and inspire meaningful actions.

In conclusion, the Earthizens Revolution 2050 introduces innovative research constructions that could now be further explored to enhance global sustainability. Personalized constitutions for Homizens, powered by AI, align individual and family goals with the Sustainable Development Goals (SDGs), fostering a harmonious and supportive environment. This initiative categorizes homes as fit or fat based on their resource utilization, emphasizing the importance of sustainable practices. Supported by the GOLA Foundation, families can track their progress through stages of Homizenship, ultimately achieving Earthizenship.

This journey empowers families to contribute significantly to global well-being, with exceptional families recognized as Earthizens of Eminence. The Constitution of Earthizens further prepares us to unite against global threats, ensuring our collective efforts are aligned and effective. These constructions offer a promising foundation for future research, aiming to build a brighter, more sustainable future for all.

# SECTION D

# Re-imagined: Role of Global Universities

Our primary audience comprises 300 global universities, nominated and eventually selected on a first-enrolled, first-onboard basis, as per the terms and conditions set by the Foundation. These universities could play a pivotal role in shaping the future of our planet. The finalization process is designed to ensure diverse representation from various geographical regions and populations.

All universities will have an enrollment donation, which can either be paid by the university's management or sponsored by their registered alumni. There will also be an additional annual fee for maintaining membership in this prestigious group with significant responsibilities. The first university to join will donate Rs 1,00,000 INR, with each subsequent joining university paying an additional Rs 1,00,000 INR, up to Rs 3,00,00,000 INR for the last. Contributions will be in INR only, and initial membership will last until 2036. After this period, the bottom 10% of inactive universities will be declared emeritus, and the next set of interested universities will be invited at a cost above Rs 3,00,00,000 INR, increasing by Rs 1,00,000 INR each. This exercise will repeat every alternate year, starting in 2036, or as decided by the management. Currently, the first three universities have already contributed their part from the first batch of thirty we were open to registering.

If an alumnus sponsors the Chair for their university, that Chair could be named after the alumnus, ensuring that the contribution is duly acknowledged. The responsibility of who attends the annual conference for representation will remain with the university.

They will be represented either by an alumni couple or by designated heads for this task, ideally as married couples who are parents with two or more children, with at least one of them having been associated with the university for a long time. This approach, as a stringent condition, ensures that families of four or more (including pets) join these self-funded sessions, so the cost isn't a burden on the university, for the annual offline global gatherings close to Christmas.

Here, they rediscover, understand, unlearn, edit, change, or transform the future Earthizens in a way that is family growth centric. By involving families, we emphasize the importance of nurturing and educating the next generation, help make and modify rules for the future required for better transition from Homizens to Earthizens in a holistic and inclusive way. This exercise would be as much about being parents and happily married couples, as it is about being Homizens and Earthizens.

These 300 universities, their leaders, their alumni, and their representative families will be the torchbearers of the Earthizens Revolution, leading by example and fostering a culture of sustainability within their institutions, families, and beyond. They will be responsible for promoting sustainable practices, collaborating on global initiatives, and driving the transition from Homizens to Earthizens. Let us not forget, it all starts from our own homes.

**Significance of Alumni Leadership:** Alumni taking the lead in such initiatives is of immense significance. Their involvement brings a wealth of experience, credibility, and a deep connection to their alma mater. Alumni can leverage their professional networks and resources to support and enhance not only the university's sustainability efforts but also share the larger vision on such annual platforms to showcase what they are observing and believe in. Their representation ensures that the initiatives are grounded in real-world experience and practical knowledge. Moreover, alumni sponsorships can inspire current students and faculty, fostering a culture of giving back and community engagement.

By naming Chairs after alumni sponsors, we not only honor their contributions but also create lasting legacies that motivate others to follow suit. Alumni-led initiatives can drive innovation, secure funding, and build strong partnerships, ultimately contributing to the success and impact of the Earthizens Revolution. One university could have more than one such Chair, and these Chairs could represent the annual gatherings by rotation. Their active participation underscores the importance of lifelong commitment to education and sustainability, reinforcing the idea that the journey from Homizens to Earthizens is a collective and continuous effort.

# SECTION E

# Exploring Re-imagined Mindset

The "XYZ mindset" embodies a holistic approach to life, emphasizing adaptability, curiosity, and innovation. It represents the end of the journey, focusing on the conclusion of each creation to ensure wise use of resources. Transitioning from a Homizen to an Earthizen involves adopting various lenses—Earning, Saving, Legal, Ethical, Consumption, Wastage, and Recycling—to promote a sustainable and ethical existence. This mindset encourages mindful actions that align with environmental and social responsibility, fostering a culture of sustainability and growth. Let us explore how the XYZ mindset can transform our approach to life and the world around us.

## Thought behind XYZ mindset

The "XYZ mindset" could be interpreted in various ways, depending on the context. Here are a few possible meanings:

1. Variable and adaptable mindset: In algebra, XYZ represents variables or unknowns. This mindset could symbolize being open to change, adaptable, and willing to navigate uncertainty.

2. Exploratory and experimental mindset: XYZ might represent the unknown or unexplored. This mindset could embody a sense of curiosity, experimentation, and innovation.

3. Analytical and problem-solving mindset: In mathematics and science, XYZ often represents coordinates or dimensions. This mindset could signify a methodical, analytical approach to problem-solving and critical thinking.

4. Unconventional and creative mindset: The term "XYZ" might imply a departure from conventional thinking (ABC for beginners). This mindset could celebrate unconventional ideas, creative thinking, and outside-the-box problem-solving.

Our interpretation of the XYZ mindset is simpler. By focusing on the end of the journey, as represented by the last letters of the English alphabet, we ensure that we understand the conclusion of each creation. This allows us to use resources wisely.

To build on that, let us observe how transitioning from a Homizen to an Earthizen involves adopting a holistic approach to life.

This means considering various lenses to ensure a sustainable and ethical existence.

Through the Earning Lens, one focuses on generating income in ways that are environmentally friendly and socially responsible. The Saving Lens emphasizes the importance of conserving resources and finances for future generations, aligning with the principle of sustainability. Viewing life through the Legal Lens ensures that all actions comply with laws designed to protect the environment and society. The Ethical Lens guides decisions based on moral principles, promoting fairness and respect for all living beings. The Consumption Lens encourages mindful consumption, reducing unnecessary purchases and opting for eco-friendly products. The Wastage Lens highlights the need to minimize waste, advocating for efficient use of resources. Finally, the Recycling Lens underscores the importance of reusing materials to reduce the environmental footprint.

By integrating these lenses into our daily lives, we can effectively transition from Homizens to Earthizens, fostering a culture of sustainability and ethical living. This holistic approach ensures that every action we take is mindful of its impact on the planet and future generations.

We see all these as part of the proposed mindset expressed as the XYZ mindset, in its different avatars. Let us now observe these mindsets under few different lenses.

## XYZ Consumer

Making conscious choices that prioritize sustainability involves selecting environmentally friendly products and considering their end-of-life impact. Consumers need to be aware that anything created either gets buried or burnt, contributing to pollution. By reducing waste and supporting companies that adhere to sustainable practices, consumers can minimize their environmental footprint. The responsibility for every kilogram of product purchased needs to be clearly defined. This extends to recycling and properly disposing of products to ensure they do not harm the planet, emphasizing the importance of mindful spending.

We often wonder why there is so little respect for used clothes and items. Why can't we create valid, practical certificates for refurbishing and promoting those who use such items? Why is buying new considered fashionable while wearing old is not? It's all designed to make us consume more, benefiting large companies. While that may be fair from a business perspective, it's not when viewed from the standpoint of our only known heaven, Earth. These thoughts often cross the mind of the XYZ consumer.

## XYZ Producer

Creating products and services that are environmentally friendly requires producers to innovate and develop solutions that minimize environmental impact. Producers must consider the entire lifecycle of their products, from production to disposal. By using sustainable materials and processes, they can reduce the likelihood of products ending up in landfills or being incinerated. Producers play a crucial role in promoting sustainability by designing products that are durable, recyclable, and biodegradable.

## XYZ Employee

Advocating for sustainable practices within the workplace involves promoting eco-friendly policies and reducing resource consumption. Employees can drive change by encouraging their colleagues to adopt sustainable habits and by being mindful of the environmental impact of their actions. This includes reducing paper usage, conserving energy, and supporting workplace recycling programs. Employees should feel responsible for the end-of-life impact of the products and services they help create. To take it further as a formal research we have proposed Polo strategy for sustainability, which has been expressed in greater details, in the appendices.

## XYZ Investor

Supporting businesses and initiatives that align with the Sustainable Development Goals (SDGs) is essential for investors who want to contribute to environmental conservation and sustainability. Investors should prioritize funding projects that have a positive environmental impact and consider the long-term sustainability of their investments. By backing companies that focus on reducing waste and promoting sustainable practices, investors can help ensure that the products and services they support do not end up harming the planet. This approach is often referred to as XYZ Green Investing, in our circle. After all, being an investor stands for earning time, and if one can invest that time well in fitness, it could lead to a longer, healthier life on Earth.

## XYZ Researcher

Conducting research that advances our understanding of sustainability involves exploring new technologies, methods, and strategies to address environmental challenges. Researchers must consider the end-of-life impact of the innovations they develop and strive to create solutions that are sustainable and environmentally friendly. By focusing on reducing waste and promoting recycling, researchers can contribute to a more sustainable future.

## XYZ Educator

Teaching and promoting sustainable practices is a key responsibility for educators. They must impart knowledge about environmental issues and inspire the next generation to become Earthizens who are aware of the end-of-life impact of the products they use. Educators should emphasize the importance of reducing waste, recycling, and supporting sustainable practices to ensure that students understand their role in protecting the planet.

Additionally, educators can foster the XYZ mindset by encouraging learners to share knowledge and resources selflessly, especially with those who cannot reciprocate. They could also instill the importance of integrity, teaching students to be true to their word both to themselves and their communities. This approach helps cultivate honest, selfless learners who promptly acknowledge their mistakes and learn from them. This is the essence of being a great student under the guidance of a top-class educator.

## XYZ Adolescence

Parents play a crucial role in guiding their children through the XYZ phase of adolescence by observing the 24 "spokes" of development, akin to the Ashoka Chakra in India's flag, and identifying any gaps. This involves recognizing strengths in academics, social skills, and emotional intelligence, while pinpointing areas needing improvement. Often, the guidance parents provide as finishing touches can be mistaken for internal conflict. Celebrating progress with positive reinforcement builds confidence and resilience. This balanced approach ensures adolescents develop into well-rounded individuals, ready to face adulthood's challenges and evolve into responsible Earthizens.

## XYZ Couples

Why only 'Kanyaa Daan' in a typical wedding? Why not 'Pootra Daan' alongside, to ensure that the couple becomes the responsibility of the Earth, to whom then both get gifted? This way they become the responsibility of all Gods on Earth, including those which the couple & their families have more hope or faith in.

Why isn't the age for marriage set at 24, considering that humans of all genders take time to mature these days? How about requiring an oath on the Constitution for those who marry, regardless of their religion? Why do some women change their names after marriage? As couples in a marriage, one of the key expectations from planet Earth is to help sustain the human population and ensure the flow of DNA continues. Shouldn't that be the focus? Many such earthy questions need to be answered to provide the deserving respect to more on our Earth.

Another question that arises is the surname children would carry, if the mother decides not to change her name after marriage. They could either toss a coin to decide which grandparent's name to use or keep a surname that combines both parents' names. For XYZ couples, a few things become clearer: the marriage is successful with the forwarding of DNA, irrespective of which family's name gets forwarded. Also, for them, the day they met is more auspicious than any other day, including the date when they got married, as everything else happened because that first day happened. The rest needs to evolve as XYZ couples are a future trend, taking shape and form over time.

## XYZ Eater

Choosing diets that are sustainable and environmentally friendly involves conscious consumption, opting for locally sourced and organic foods, and minimizing food waste. Eaters should be aware of the environmental impact of their food choices and strive to reduce their carbon footprint. By composting food scraps and supporting sustainable agriculture, eaters can help ensure that their dietary habits do not contribute to environmental degradation. Focusing on the ABC of eating—whether one is vegetarian, non-vegetarian, or vegan is traditional. However, it is equally crucial to understand the XYZ of eating, which involves fulfilling the body's nutritional needs for vitamins, carbohydrates, proteins, minerals, fats, water and other essential nutrients. This holistic perspective on diet and nutrition needs global awareness to promote both personal health and environmental sustainability.

## XYZ Believer

Embracing a philosophy that prioritizes the planet involves advocating for environmental stewardship and inspiring others to adopt a sustainable lifestyle. Believers should be mindful of the end-of-life impact of the products they use and promote practices that reduce waste and pollution.

For instance, consider the old belief that the tree wood used for one's final rites, as in Hinduism, could be more ideal if it is grown by the person for whom the wood is used, within that person's lifetime or by their family. This can now be easily achieved using modern technology such as drones, GPS, QR codes, and Digital Aadhaar for Trees. This approach presents a significant solopreneurship opportunity for farmers with small pieces of land. By ensuring the tree is grown by the user's representative in the village and nurtured through digital means, we can create a sustainable cycle that benefits both the individual and the community.

By leading by example and encouraging others to make sustainable choices, believers can help drive the Earthizens Revolution. This movement aims to foster a global commitment to living in harmony with the planet, ensuring a better future for all.

## XYZ Sports

Ever wondered why sports were even created? The XYZ of sports is fitness, yet we increasingly see a focus on winning and the loss of egos. Imagine a cricket match where, instead of just runs and wickets, we use technology to calculate the steps taken and the energy burned as criteria for winning. This approach would emphasize the physical fitness and effort of the players, rather than just the final score.

XYZ Sports aims to revolutionize the way we perceive and engage in sports. By integrating advanced fitness tracking technologies, we can shift the focus back to the core values of sports: health, fitness, and teamwork. Players would be motivated to maintain peak physical condition, knowing that their efforts are being measured and rewarded.

Moreover, this approach could extend beyond professional sports. Imagine community leagues and school sports programs adopting these metrics, promoting a culture of health and fitness from a young age. Parents and coaches would have a new way to encourage and track the progress of young athletes, focusing on their overall development rather than just their ability to win games.

In essence, XYZ Sports seeks to redefine success in sports, making it about more than just winning. It's about celebrating the journey, the effort, and the commitment to fitness. By doing so, we can create a more positive and inclusive sports culture that values every participant's contribution. We all belong to one planet, Earth, and should celebrate fitness irrespective of nationality. As friends and family of the same Earth, anyone's loss or pain need not be the reason for others' happiness.

## XYZ Govt

Why is it that those who properly segregate waste do not receive compensation or encouragement through reduced property taxes? Why can't local governments ban dumping waste in non-designated areas by implementing intensive CCTV coverage? Additionally, they could introduce differential rates for various levels of segregated waste, measured in kilograms, linking property tax to the level of segregated waste generated by each colony. This approach could help manage the waste issue more effectively, as better-segregated waste would be produced and processed accordingly.

Further, naming and shaming those colonies, RWAs, and PINCODES that take the least advantage of waivers available for saving individual property tax could also help.

## XYZpreneurial Mindset

"Preneurial" is a combination of the words "preneur" (short for entrepreneur) and the suffix "-ial," which forms an adjective. By Definition: Preneurial_ refers to the mindset, characteristics, or behaviors typically associated with entrepreneurs, such as:

1. Innovative thinking: Embracing creativity, experimentation, and calculated risk-taking.
2. Proactivity: Taking initiative, being self-motivated, and driving change.

3.  Resilience: Adapting to challenges, learning from failures, and persevering.
4.  Visionary thinking: Having a clear vision, setting goals, and striving for growth.
5.  Adaptability: Being flexible, open to new opportunities, and able to pivot when necessary.

In essence, having a preneurial mindset means embracing the entrepreneurial spirit, whether you're starting a business, leading a team, or driving innovation within an organization. So, what exactly is an entrepreneurial mindset?

An entrepreneurial mindset refers to a particular way of thinking and approaching opportunities, challenges, and decision-making. It encompasses a set of beliefs, thought processes, and skills that enable individuals to identify and create opportunities, take calculated risks, and persist in the face of setbacks. People with an entrepreneurial mindset often foster innovation, resourcefulness, and adaptability, allowing them to navigate the complex world of business.

> However, it is essential to recognize that an entrepreneurial mindset is not limited to founders of large companies. One could be a simple employee of an organization and still embrace and build their entrepreneurial mindset. This can happen if the person is employed in an organization that has a culture of embracing, encouraging, and making the most of the entrepreneurial mindset of its employees, by acknowledging them explicitly or otherwise as intrapreneurs. On the other hand, one could simply be a single-person organization, as a solopreneur, defining the salary they wish to draw by themselves. This brings forward an opportunity to reimagine how the entrepreneurial mindset is served to those who are open to looking at it in a different light.

## The Challenge

The term "Entrepreneurial Mindset" includes the word "Entrepreneur." This makes it naturally more relatable to the word "Entrepreneur" than to other aspects of the entrepreneurship family, including intrapreneurship and solopreneurship.

All three differ significantly when it comes to the responsibility of arranging one's own salary. In the case of entrepreneurship, the key responsibility of arranging funds for the regular salary of all team members, including the entrepreneur, lies with the entrepreneur. This is similar in solopreneurship, but since it is a one-person or of a few from one family type of organization, the salary decision is more personal and depends on the individual's wishes and circumstances. The situation is completely different in intrapreneurship, where a larger organization provides the funding and support for regular planned salaries, while also considering the risks and uncertainties of running a new startup.

This is similar to the story of Shri Ramlal, who has three sons: one named Ramlal, and the other two named Mohanlal and Shyamlal. When the neighbors' kids shout out for Mohanlal or Shyamlal, they understand they are being addressed. However, confusion arises when the call is for Ramlal. The same issue occurs with marriage proposals for Ramlal. No wonder Ramlal the father is married, while Ramlal the son is still waiting, as the confusion has caused him great damage.

Similar confusions exist in families with common names. For instance, consider the family of David Johnson, who has two sons named David and Johnson. When someone calls out for David, both father and son might respond, leading to misunderstandings. This can be particularly problematic in situations like school registrations, medical appointments, or even social gatherings. Johnson, on the other hand, might face similar issues when his name is called out, especially if there are other Johnsons in the vicinity.

By understanding these examples, we can see how common names across generations can lead to significant confusion and impact various aspects of life. The story of entrepreneurship is similar, as it encompasses various dimensions such as intrapreneurship, solopreneurship, entrepreneurship and more, all under its larger umbrella called Entrepreneurship.

Similar are probably the perceptions of family members of those who wish to work towards an entrepreneurial mindset. The family, friends, and well-wishers that the individual interacts with are truly afraid of this person becoming dependent on them if the regularity of cash flow isn't planned, which people generally relate closely with the word "entrepreneurship." The situation sometimes becomes so grave, with most entrepreneurial ventures closing down, that parents start to wonder if entrepreneurship is a fall they are pushing their kids to or is it a climb that they wish the kids to experience.

To get to a possible solution and a resolution, let us look at the analogies for intrapreneurship, solopreneurship, and entrepreneurship:

**Solopreneurship:** This could be likened to marathon running. Just as a marathon runner relies solely on their own endurance, strategy, and determination to complete the race, a solopreneur depends on their individual skills, resilience, and self-motivation to drive their business forward. The solitary nature of marathon running reflects the independence and self-reliance required in solopreneurship, where success hinges on personal effort and perseverance.

**Intrapreneurship:** This could be likened to polo. Just as polo players depend on their horses for agility, speed, and coordination, intrapreneurs rely on the resources, support, and infrastructure of their organization to innovate and drive new initiatives within the company. The synergy between the player and the horse mirrors the collaboration between an intrapreneur and their corporate environment, enabling them to navigate challenges and achieve goals effectively.

**Entrepreneurship:** This might be compared to football (soccer). In football, success depends on teamwork, strategy, and coordination among players, much like entrepreneurship relies on collaboration, diverse skill sets, and collective effort to achieve business goals. The dynamic interplay between team members in football illustrates the importance of networking, leadership, and shared vision in entrepreneurship, where the combined strengths of the team propel the business towards success.

Intrapreneurship, solopreneurship, and entrepreneurship each embody unique dynamics similar to different sports. As expressed above, Intrapreneurship is like polo, relying on organizational support; solopreneurship mirrors marathon running, emphasizing individual effort; and entrepreneurship resembles football, thriving on teamwork. Together, they highlight the diverse paths to innovation and success in the business world.

## Re-imagining the Entrepreneurial Mindset

The traditional entrepreneurial mindset, while powerful, often overlooks certain aspects that can be crucial for sustainable and inclusive growth. The XYZpreneurial mindset addresses these gaps by integrating innovation, sustainability, and inclusivity into the core of entrepreneurial thinking.

Central to the Earthizens Revolution 2050 is the concept of the XYZpreneurial mindset. This innovative approach encourages individuals to question the status quo and adopt sustainable practices in every aspect of their lives, while being open to receiving a salary for innovations and transformations they propose and execute.

The XYZpreneurial mindset encompasses various roles, enabling Homizens to evolve into Earthizens by embracing the XYZ phase in multiple ways. This evolution requires a new language for recognition and a new taxonomy, so let's understand that now.

## XYZ TAXONOMY for Sustainable Ventures

The term "XYZ TAXONOMY for Sustainable Ventures" refers to a classification system designed to categorize and define various types of sustainable entrepreneurial activities. This taxonomy aims to provide a structured framework for understanding and promoting sustainable business practices. Here are some key aspects:

**Classification System:** This new taxonomy would classify different types of sustainable ventures based on specific criteria. These criteria could include the uniqueness they offer, referred to as the X Factor; alignment with the Sustainable Development Goals (SDGs), expressed as the Y Factor, which answers the "why" question; and clarity on the type of enterprise (Solo, Intra, or Entre), known as the Z Factor, which answers the "how" and "who" questions.

**XYZpreneurial Mindset:** The taxonomy integrates the XYZ Mindset and entrepreneurial mindset and thereby encourages individuals to adopt sustainable practices in various roles, such as consumers, producers, employees, investors, researchers, educators, and more. This mindset emphasizes the importance of sustainability in every aspect of entrepreneurial ventures.

**Ashram Name:** Inspired by the Indian concept of ashrams, this taxonomy categorizes sustainable ventures into different "ashrams" or groups based on their focus and impact. For example, an entrepreneurial venture focused on sustainable agriculture might be classified under the "Organic Agri Entre ~ Ashram," while an intrapreneurial venture promoting renewable energy could fall under the "Solar Energy Intra ~ Ashram."

**Sustainable Practices:** The taxonomy highlights the importance of adopting sustainable practices in all entrepreneurial activities irrespective of the stage where the venture currently is in. This includes reducing waste, using eco-friendly materials, supporting fair trade, and promoting ethical business practices.

**Global Collaboration:** By providing a clear and structured classification system, the new taxonomy aims to facilitate global collaboration and investment in sustainable ventures. It helps investors, policymakers, and venture capitalists identify and support businesses that contribute to a sustainable future. This system significantly aids in bringing together people facing similar issues, making it easier to obtain information straight from the horse's mouth. This perspective could be a game changer, offering relevant opportunities and support to teams working on specific SDGs in the medium to long term.

Overall, the "XYZ TAXONOMY for Sustainable Ventures" is a comprehensive framework that promotes sustainability, innovation, and global cooperation in the entrepreneurial ecosystem.

It is important to note that various prefixes have been added to the common word "preneurial," which is used in different contexts to express an entrepreneurial focus with various functions. This includes terms like entrepreneurial, intrapreneurial, solopreneurial, edupreneur, techpreneur, mathspreneur, agripreneur, and toypreneur. By using the 'XYZ' prefix in its expanded form, we can create a bundle of unified, globally acceptable terms that encompass all these variations, making it easier to communicate the diverse nature of entrepreneurial activities on our planet Earth. All these variations could be covered by the XYZ Taxonomy.

Further, by using the term "XYZpreneurial mindset" instead of "entrepreneurial mindset" simplifies communication with upcoming entrepreneurs, their families and other role holders. It clarifies that one could even expect a salary while working towards building an entrepreneurial mindset, making it more inclusive and relatable. This approach helps in breaking down the barriers and misconceptions about entrepreneurship, encouraging more people to adopt this mindset. It has various differentiators but the below are the key:

**Salary Inclusion:** The new term emphasizes that the XYZpreneurial mindset includes those who receive a salary, not just those who provide one. This distinction is important for young adults and their families as they prepare to support the next generation with education and grooming, ensuring they can meet their responsibilities despite limited resources. By acknowledging the realities of life, we can create a more supportive environment for aspiring entrepreneurs.

**Loans and Liabilities:** Debt repayment is a significant obstacle for many entrepreneurs, especially as their businesses face challenges. Loans and liabilities are integral to business operations due to scarce capital. Managing debt while navigating a growing business adds complexity to the entrepreneurial journey. Understanding this financial dimension is crucial for developing strategies to mitigate risks and ensure long-term success.

**Intrapreneurship Financing:** Intrapreneurship is generally better financed than entrepreneurship because it typically has the backing of a larger company. However, more data is needed to express this with greater confidence. The financial support available to intrapreneurs can make a significant difference in their success, highlighting the importance of securing adequate funding for entrepreneurial ventures. This interdependence between financial stability and entrepreneurial success underscores the need for comprehensive financial planning.

The XYZpreneurial mindset also emphasizes focusing on the end rather than just the beginning. This approach encourages entrepreneurs to consider different roles and the ultimate impact of their ventures on our planet and beyond. By keeping the end goal in mind, entrepreneurs can better navigate the challenges and opportunities that arise along their journey, ensuring that their efforts lead to meaningful and sustainable outcomes.

## XYZ Ashram Name

The term "Ashram Name" is created for sustainable entrepreneurship ventures that have SDGs as part of their key strategy, by the author of this book. The term "Ashram" also connects with the Sanskrit word for a place of meditation, emphasizing the spiritual and the much-needed journey by sustainable ventures. This new taxonomy aims to suggest a sense of identity and purpose for sustainable entrepreneurs, whose mission is not just to earn profits but also to ensure that the element of sustainability is honored.

> The new taxonomy, akin to scientific literature, will succinctly describe and inquire about the enterprise. This approach aims to make listeners more aware of how the venture contributes to our Earth, categorizing ventures with specific prefixes and referring to the mindset as the XYZpreneurial Mindset. By adopting a scientific approach, we can create a structured and systematic way of understanding and promoting sustainable ventures. Therefore, this new method of addressing truly needs further research, as it could ensure that more and more sustainable ventures identify the ashram they belong to, thereby allowing their resources to have a voice, a structure, and recognition for the global audience to appreciate.

When identifying their venture, entrepreneurs can use the XYZpreneurial mindset to specify their Ashram. For instance, a MathsPreneur would belong to the Maths-Edu-Entre-Preneur Ashram. This identification helps in understanding the unique focus of each venture and fosters a sense of belonging and purpose within their specific entrepreneurial community. This brings us to understanding in detail how the XYZ Ashram name is decoded.

> **X Part of the Ashram Name:** The X factor represents what makes an enterprise unique. It answers questions like what, which, where, and when, highlighting the distinctiveness or uniqueness that sets the enterprise apart. For instance, an entrepreneur in the educational toys business could be described as a Toy-Edu-Entre-Preneur, clearly expressing their focus. The X factor is crucial for differentiating ventures and emphasizing their unique value propositions.

> **Y Part of the Ashram Name:** The Y part of the XYZpreneurial Mindset represents the 17 defined Sustainable Development Goals (SDGs) that inspire sustainable entrepreneurial teams to advance their ventures. These SDGs are described with one-word terms: Poverty, Hunger, Health, Education, Equality, Water, Energy, Work, Industry, Inequality, Cities,

Consumption, Climate, Oceans, Land, Justice, and Partnerships. An additional option called "others," which could even be referred to as "GLOBAL," is available in case more than one aspect is addressed by the venture. This comprehensive approach ensures all potential areas of impact are considered, promoting a holistic view of sustainability. This part answers the question "Why?" of the sustainability venture. Additionally, the similarity in sound between 'Y' and 'Why' makes it easy to relate and connect.

**Z Part of the Ashram Name:** The Z part of the XYZpreneurial Mindset encompasses one of three approaches: solopreneurship, intrapreneurship, or entrepreneurship. This section extends the 'Why' question with a deeper focus on 'Who & How'. The 'Why' is often embedded within the Who and How the venture is planned, especially regarding sustainability. The 'Who' refers to the individuals or teams driving the venture, their skills, values, and vision. The 'How' involves the methods, processes, and innovations they employ to achieve their objectives.

> By understanding who is behind the venture and how they are implementing their strategies, we can uncover the deeper motivations and goals that define the 'Why'. This holistic approach ensures that the sustainability goals are not just theoretical but are actively pursued through practical and impactful actions.

The Z part, therefore, provides a robust framework for analyzing and enhancing the effectiveness of sustainable ventures, emphasizing that the 'Why' is intrinsically linked to the 'Who' and 'How'.

By understanding these distinctions, we can better appreciate the diverse ways in which entrepreneurial activities could be structured to understand and communicate their significance, role & needs better.

> **Solopreneurship:** In solopreneurship, the promoter is the only person involved, meaning they are likely the only one receiving a salary. Couplepreneurship is an extension of this concept, involving mainly one or a few individuals working together. This category highlights the independence and self-reliance of solopreneurs, who often manage all aspects of their business on their own. Solopreneurs must be versatile and resourceful, handling everything from marketing to finance. This includes social media influencers, proprietor, single person shops, pop mom stores and many with similar traits.

> **Intrapreneurship:** Intrapreneurship involves individuals who are intrapreneurial but receive a salary from an employer. This category highlights the employment structure where the individual works within a larger organization, leveraging its resources and support to

drive innovation and growth. Intrapreneurs benefit from the stability and backing of their employer while pursuing entrepreneurial initiatives. They often act as change agents within their organizations, fostering a culture of innovation.

**Entrepreneurship:** Entrepreneurship involves individuals who are primarily responsible for expanding the business and providing salaries to employees. Entrepreneurs take on significant risks and responsibilities, including financial risk, potential losses, business closures, and compliance with regulations. They must navigate complex business environments, ensuring their ventures remain viable and compliant with legal standards. Entrepreneurs shoulder a lot from the beginning, driving the vision and growth of their ventures while managing the financial health and operational stability of their businesses. Their role is crucial in job creation and economic development, often bringing new products and services to market. Entrepreneurs must be strategic thinkers, capable of handling the multifaceted challenges of running a business.

In conclusion, the XYZpreneurial mindset is a transformative approach that integrates Innovation, sustainability and inclusivity. By adopting this mindset, individuals and organizations can contribute to a more sustainable and equitable future, aligning their entrepreneurial efforts with the broader goals of the Earthizens Revolution 2050.

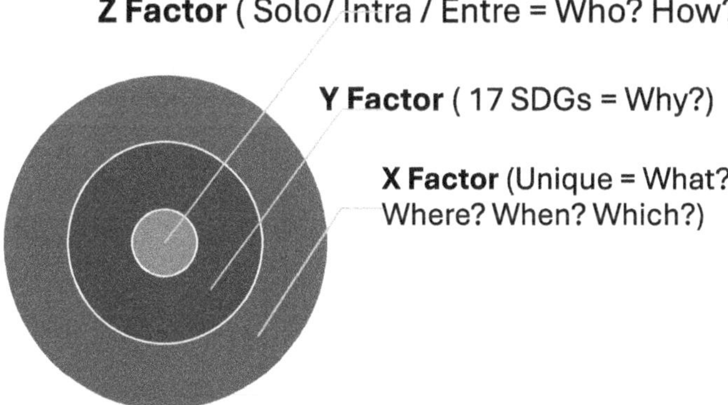


*Figure 1: For XYZ Taxonomy for Sustainable Ventures ~ Diagram*

# SECTION F

# Exploring Re-imagined Path to SDGs by AI

The journey from Homizens to Earthizens involves a fundamental shift in mindset and behavior. Homizens, or citizens at home and in family, are encouraged to embrace the principles of sustainability and become active participants in the Earthizens Revolution 2050, re-imagining the path to achieving the SDGs.

In the intricate tapestry of human civilization, the home has always been the fundamental unit of society. A family, living harmoniously, nurturing values, and fostering development within the confines of their home, gives rise to good Homizens – citizens who embody the virtues of kindness, empathy, responsibility, and respect within their immediate surroundings. But in a world increasingly interconnected and facing global challenges, it's time to reimagine our identities and responsibilities beyond the four walls of our homes. It's time for Homizens to evolve into Earthizens.

With that, a good Homizen is the cornerstone of any strong community. These individuals uphold moral values, respect their family members, contribute to household duties, and ensure a nurturing environment for all. They teach and practice sustainability, waste management, and energy conservation at home, setting an example for the younger generation. Their actions within the home reflect the principles of a just, respectful, and caring society.

As the challenges of climate change, global health crises, and political instability loom large, there is an urgent need for these values to extend beyond our homes and into the wider world. This transformation from Homizen to Earthizen involves a conscious effort to scale the principles of respect, empathy, and responsibility to a global level.

Earthizenship envisions individuals who are committed to the well-being of our planet and its inhabitants. This new identity acknowledges that while we may come from diverse cultures, religions, and regions, we share a common home – Earth. Earthizens take collective action to address global issues, advocate for sustainable practices, and promote peace and unity.

Key pillars of Earthizenship could be considered as below:

1.  **Global Responsibility:** Earthizens understand that their actions affect people and ecosystems worldwide. They practice sustainable living and advocate for policies that protect the environment.

2.  **Cultural Empathy:** Earthizens celebrate diversity and promote inclusivity. They are open-minded and respectful towards different cultures, fostering global unity.

3.  **Community Engagement:** Earthizens actively participate in local and global communities. They volunteer, support grassroots movements, and engage in dialogue to solve global problems.

4.  **Lifelong Learning:** Earthizens are committed to continuous education and awareness about global issues. They stay informed and adapt to new challenges with innovative solutions.

In a rapidly changing world, the evolution from Homizen to Earthizen is not just desirable, but essential. By expanding the scope of our responsibilities from our homes to our planet, we can create a more just, sustainable, and peaceful world. This transformation begins with the individual but requires collective action and global cooperation.

As Earthizens, we can rise to meet the challenges of the future, united by our shared humanity and our common home, Earth.

## Researchable Solutions by AI

Homizens are encouraged to integrate sustainable practices into their daily lives and community activities, making small yet meaningful actions that collectively have a significant impact on the environment. By practicing conscious consumption, supporting ethical businesses, and advocating for policies that align with the Sustainable Development Goals (SDGs), Homizens can drive substantial change. For instance, reducing water usage, supporting clean energy initiatives, and promoting responsible consumption are practical steps that contribute to the SDGs. Additionally, volunteering for community projects, educating others about sustainability, and participating in local and global campaigns further amplify their efforts.

These actions not only foster a culture of sustainability but also help Homizens transition to Earthizens, symbolizing a higher level of consciousness and responsibility towards the planet.

The Earthizens Revolution 2050 emphasizes the importance of these daily acts, encouraging Homizens to take proactive steps in their personal and community lives. By integrating these practices, Homizens can make a significant impact on the environment and contribute to the global mission of achieving the SDGs, ultimately fostering a sustainable and resilient future for all.

*Let us look at each of the 17 Sustainable Development Goals (SDGs) one by one and explore how families can contribute in their own small ways to make a difference. These ideas below as presented in italics were generated by providing suitable prompts to Copilot AI, leveraging artificial intelligence to re-imagine these solutions.*

### Goal 1: No Poverty

*1. Donate unused items to local charities.*
*2. Support local businesses and fair-trade products.*
*3. Volunteer at community centers.*
*4. Educate children about financial literacy.*
*5. Participate in community fundraising events.*
*6. Share surplus food with neighbors.*
*7. Advocate for policies that support low-income families.*
*8. Offer skills training to those in need.*
*9. Buy from social enterprises.*
*10. Reduce personal waste to lower living costs.*

*The journey from homizen to earthizen involves each family member playing a crucial role in embracing Sustainable Development Goal 1: No Poverty. This transformation is about fostering a collective mindset that prioritizes poverty alleviation, community support, and sustainable practices. By engaging in specific acts, families can significantly contribute to reducing poverty and promoting economic equity, ultimately becoming proactive Earthizens.*

*Elders: Elders in the family can lead by example in advocating for supportive policies and offering skills training. They can initiate monthly advocacy actions, such as writing letters to local representatives or participating in community meetings to promote policies that support poverty alleviation. Additionally, elders can offer skills training to individuals in the community, sharing their expertise and knowledge to help others develop valuable skills. Their wisdom and experience can provide valuable guidance and encouragement, helping trainees build confidence and resilience. Elders can also educate the family about financial literacy through weekly sessions, discussing the importance of budgeting, saving, and investing wisely.*

*Parents: Parents are instrumental in promoting community support and supporting local businesses. They can actively participate in community fundraising events by organizing family outings to local events that focus on poverty alleviation and community support. This quarterly activity of participating in at least one fundraising* event can instill a sense of responsibility towards promoting economic equity in children. Furthermore, parents can support local businesses by making conscious choices about the products they purchase. This could include buying from local shops and educating the family about the impact of their purchasing decisions. Through these actions, parents demonstrate the importance of supporting local economies, guiding their family towards becoming responsible Earthizens.

Kids: Children, with their boundless energy and curiosity, can be champions of donating unused items and reducing personal waste. They can participate in monthly actions that promote donation, such as collecting and donating unused items to local charities. These activities help children understand and appreciate the importance of sharing and supporting those in need. Additionally, kids can reduce personal waste by learning about sustainable alternatives and encouraging their peers to make environmentally conscious choices. These experiences teach children the value of minimizing waste and instill a sense of responsibility towards creating a sustainable society.

Family Activities: As a cohesive unit, families can engage in activities that promote awareness about poverty alleviation and share surplus food. Weekly sessions where the family discusses the importance of sharing surplus food and the impact of dietary choices on the community can be enlightening. These discussions, facilitated by parents or elders, can involve interactive activities like cooking together or sharing meals to make learning engagement for kids. Supporting initiatives that promote poverty alleviation is another area where families can contribute collectively. Monthly actions such as volunteering at community centers or buying from social enterprises help raise awareness and promote sustainable practices within the community.

Collective Advocacy: Families can advocate poverty alleviation by participating in campaigns that highlight the importance of promoting economic equity and community support. This could involve writing letters to local representatives or joining advocacy groups that work towards establishing and maintaining supportive policies. By engaging in these activities together, families reinforce the values of sustainability and economic equity. Promoting awareness about poverty alleviation within the family, educating financial literacy, and supporting local businesses are foundational steps in this journey. Each family member, from elders to kids, contributes uniquely to these efforts, creating a ripple effect that extends beyond the household.

The Path to Earthizenship: The journey from homizen to earthizen is marked by a series of transformative actions that align with the Earthizens Revolution 2050. By donating unused items, families cultivate a culture of sharing and responsibility.

*Supporting local businesses and participating in community fundraising events instills a deep sense of commitment to promoting economic equality. Advocating supportive policies and educating about financial literacy empowers families to be active participants in their communities. Volunteering at community centers, sharing surplus food, and reducing personal waste foster a sense of global Earthizenship and responsibility.*

*As families engage in these acts, they transition from being homizens—citizens of their homes—to Earthizens, proactive global citizens committed to poverty alleviation. This transformation is not just about individual actions but about fostering a collective mindset that aligns with global sustainability and economic equity. By embracing these practices, families contribute to reducing poverty and promoting economic equity, ultimately achieving the vision of a harmonious and sustainable world.*

*In summary, the journey from homizen to earthizen is a transformative process that involves every family member. Elders provide wisdom and guidance, parents advocate and engage in community activities, and children champion sustainable practices and community support. Together, families educate about financial literacy, reduce personal waste, and advocate for supportive policies. Through these collective efforts, homizens evolve into Earthizens, contributing to a sustainable and harmonious world. This journey is a call to action for families to unite and create a better future for all.*

Goal 1: No Poverty

| Act | Measurement Metric | Frequency | Target |
|---|---|---|---|
| Donate unused items | Number of items donated | Monthly | 10 items/month |
| Support local businesses | Amount spent on local products | Weekly | ₹1000/week |
| Volunteer at community centers | Hours volunteered | Monthly | 5 hours/month |
| Educating children about financial literacy | Number of sessions | Weekly | 1 session/week |
| Participating in community fundraising events | Number of events attended | Quarterly | 1 event/quarter |
| Share surplus food | Number of meals shared | Weekly | 2 meals/week |
| Advocate for supportive policies | Number of advocacy actions | Monthly | 2 actions/month |

| Act | Measurement Metric | Frequency | Target |
|---|---|---|---|
| Offer skills training | Number of people trained | Quarterly | 3 people/quarter |
| Buy from social enterprises | Amount spent | Monthly | ₹500/month |
| Reduce personal waste | Amount of waste reduced | Monthly | 10% reduction/month |

### Goal 2: Zero Hunger

1. Grow a home vegetable garden.
2. Reduce food waste by planning meals.
3. Donate non-perishable food to food banks.
4. Support local farmers' markets.
5. Participate in community-supported agriculture (CSA).
6. Educate family members about nutrition.
7. Cook meals from scratch to avoid processed foods.
8. Share excess garden produce with neighbors.
9. Advocate for school meal programs.
10. Compost food scraps to enrich soil.

The journey from homizen to earthizen involves each family member playing a crucial role in embracing Sustainable Development Goal 2: Zero Hunger. This transformation is about fostering a collective mindset that prioritizes food security, sustainable agriculture, and nutrition. By engaging in specific acts, families can significantly contribute to reducing hunger and promoting sustainable food practices, ultimately becoming proactive Earthizens.

Elders: Elders in the family can lead by example in advocating for school meal programs and educating about nutrition. They can initiate quarterly advocacy actions, such as writing letters to local representatives or participating in community meetings to promote policies that support school meal programs. Additionally, elders can educate the family about nutrition through weekly sessions, discussing the importance of balanced diets and the impact of food choices on health. Their wisdom and experience can provide valuable insights and encouragement, helping younger family members understand the significance of nutrition and inspire them to make healthy choices.

Parents: Parents are instrumental in promoting sustainable food practices and supporting local farmers' markets. They can actively participate in community-supported agriculture (CSA) by purchasing shares from local farms. This monthly activity of participating in CSA can instill a sense of responsibility towards promoting sustainable agriculture in children. Furthermore, parents can support local farmers' markets by making conscious choices about the products they purchase. This could include buying fresh produce from local farmers and educating the family about the benefits of supporting local agriculture. Through these actions, parents demonstrate the importance of sustainable food practices, guiding their family towards becoming responsible Earthizens.

Kids: Children, with their boundless energy and curiosity, can be champions of growing a home vegetable garden and reducing food waste. They can participate in monthly actions that promote gardening, such as planting and tending to vegetables in a home garden. These activities help children understand and appreciate the importance of growing their own food and the joy of gardening. Additionally, kids can reduce food waste by learning about sustainable alternatives and encouraging their peers to make environmentally conscious choices. These experiences teach children the value of minimizing waste and instill a sense of responsibility towards creating a sustainable society.

Family Activities: As a cohesive unit, families can engage in activities that promote awareness about zero hunger and cook meals from scratch. Weekly sessions where the family discusses the importance of cooking meals from scratch and the impact of dietary choices on the environment can be enlightening. These discussions, facilitated by parents or elders, can involve interactive activities like cooking together or sharing recipes to make learning engaging for kids. Supporting initiatives that promote zero hunger is another area where families can contribute collectively. Monthly actions such as donating non-perishable food or sharing garden produce help raise awareness and promote sustainable food practices within the community.

Collective Advocacy: Families can advocate for zero hunger by participating in campaigns that highlight the importance of promoting food security and sustainable agriculture. This could involve writing letters to local representatives or joining advocacy groups that work towards establishing and maintaining food security policies. By engaging in these activities together, families reinforce the values of sustainability and food security. Promoting awareness about zero hunger within the family, educating about nutrition, and supporting local farmers' markets are foundational steps in this journey. Each family member, from elders to kids, contributes uniquely to these efforts, creating a ripple effect that extends beyond the household.

The Path to Earthizenship: The journey from homizen to earthizen is marked by a series of transformative actions that align with the Earthizens Revolution 2050. By growing a home vegetable garden, families cultivate a culture of environmental *stewardship and responsibility. Reducing food waste and participating in CSA instills a deep sense of commitment to promoting sustainable agriculture. Advocating for school meal programs and educating about nutrition empowers families to be active participants in their communities. Cooking meals from scratch, supporting local farmers' markets, and composting food scraps foster a sense of global Earthizenship and responsibility.*

*As families engage in these acts, they transition from being homizens—citizens of their homes—to Earthizens, proactive global citizens committed to zero hunger. This transformation is not just about individual actions but about fostering a collective mindset that aligns with global sustainability and food security. By embracing these practices, families contribute to reducing hunger and promoting sustainable food practices, ultimately achieving the vision of a harmonious and sustainable world.*

*In summary, the journey from homizen to earthizen is a transformative process that involves every family member. Elders provide wisdom and guidance, parents advocate and engage in community activities, and children champion sustainable practices and food security. Together, families educate about nutrition, reduce food waste, and advocate for school meal programs. Through these collective efforts, homizens evolve into Earthizens, contributing to a sustainable and harmonious world. This journey is a call to action for families to unite and create a better future for all.*

Goal 2: Zero Hunger

| Act | Measurement Metric | Frequency | Target |
| --- | --- | --- | --- |
| Grow a home vegetable garden | Number of plants grown | Monthly | 5 plants/month |
| Reduce food waste | Amount of food waste reduced | Weekly | 20% reduction/week |
| Donate non-perishable food | Number of items donated | Monthly | 10 items/month |
| Support local farmers' markets | Amount spent | Weekly | ₹500/week |
| Participate in CSA - Community-Supported Agriculture | Number of shares purchased | Monthly | 1 share/month |

| Act | Measurement Metric | Frequency | Target |
|---|---|---|---|
| Educate about nutrition | Number of sessions | Weekly | 1 session/week |
| Cook meals from scratch | Number of meals cooked | Weekly | 5 meals/week |
| Share garden produce | Amount of produce shared | Monthly | 2 kg/month |
| Advocate for school meal programs | Number of advocacy actions | Quarterly | 1 action/quarter |
| Compost food scraps | Amount of compost produced | Monthly | 5 kg/month |

### Goal 3: Good Health and Well-being

1. Exercise daily as a family.
2. Eat balanced, nutritious meals.
3. Schedule regular health check-ups.
4. Practice mindfulness or meditation.
5. Ensure adequate sleep for all family members.
6. Limit screen time and encourage outdoor activities.
7. Maintain a clean and safe home environment.
8. Educate about mental health awareness.
9. Avoid smoking and limit alcohol consumption.
10. Participate in community health initiatives.

The journey from homizen to earthizen involves each family member playing a crucial role in embracing Sustainable Development Goal 3: Good Health and Well-being. This transformation is about fostering a collective mindset that prioritizes physical health, mental well-being, and sustainable lifestyle practices. By engaging in specific acts, families can significantly contribute to promoting good health and well-being, ultimately becoming proactive Earthizens.

Elders: Elders in the family can lead by example in educating about mental health and scheduling health check-ups. They can initiate monthly sessions to discuss mental health, sharing their experiences and insights on maintaining mental well-being. These discussions can help break the stigma around mental health and encourage younger family members to seek support when needed. Additionally, elders can ensure that everyone in the family schedules regular health check-ups, emphasizing the importance of preventive care. Their wisdom and experience can provide valuable guidance on maintaining overall health and inspire younger family members to prioritize their well-being.

Parents: Parents are instrumental in promoting balanced meals and maintaining a clean home. They can actively participate in planning and preparing balanced meals, ensuring that the family consumes nutritious food daily. This daily activity of eating three balanced meals can instill healthy eating habits in children. Furthermore, parents can maintain a clean home by organizing weekly cleaning sessions. This could include tasks such as decluttering, dusting, and sanitizing common areas. Through these actions, parents demonstrate the importance of a healthy living environment, guiding their family towards becoming responsible Earthizens.

Kids: Children, with their boundless energy and curiosity, can be champions of exercising daily and limiting screen time. They can participate in daily actions that promote physical activity, such as engaging in sports, playing outside, or doing home workouts. These activities help children understand and appreciate the importance of staying active and fit. Additionally, kids can limit their screen time by setting daily limits on the use of electronic devices and finding alternative activities that do not involve screens. These experiences teach children the value of balancing screen time with other activities and instill a sense of responsibility towards maintaining their health.

Family Activities: As a cohesive unit, families can engage in activities that promote mindfulness and ensure adequate sleep. Daily sessions where the family practices mindfulness together, such as meditation or deep breathing exercises, can be enlightening. These sessions, facilitated by parents or elders, can help reduce stress and improve mental clarity. Supporting initiatives that promote good health is another area where families can contribute collectively. Quarterly actions such as participating in health initiatives or community wellness programs help raise awareness and promote healthy lifestyle practices within the community.

Collective Advocacy: Families can advocate for good health and well-being by participating in campaigns that highlight the importance of maintaining a healthy lifestyle. This could involve writing letters to local representatives or joining advocacy groups that work towards promoting health and wellness policies. By engaging in these activities together, families reinforce the values of health and well-being. Promoting awareness about mental health within the family, educating about balanced meals, and supporting health initiatives are foundational steps in this journey. Each family member, from elders to kids, contributes uniquely to these efforts, creating a ripple effect that extends beyond the household.

*The Path to Earthizenship: The journey from homizen to earthizen is marked by a series of transformative actions that align with the Earthizens Revolution 2050. By exercising daily, families cultivate a culture of physical fitness and responsibility. Eating balanced meals and participating in health initiatives instills a deep sense of commitment to promoting good health. Advocating for mental health education and practicing mindfulness empowers families to be active participants in their communities. Ensuring adequate sleep, limiting screen time, and maintaining a clean home foster a sense of global Earthizenship and responsibility.*

*As families engage in these acts, they transition from being homizens—citizens of their homes—to Earthizens, proactive global citizens committed to good health and well-being. This transformation is not just about individual actions but about fostering a collective mindset that aligns with global sustainability and health. By embracing these practices, families contribute to promoting good health and well-being, ultimately achieving the vision of a harmonious and sustainable world.*

*In conclusion, the journey from homizen to earthizen is a transformative process that involves every family member. Elders provide wisdom and guidance, parents advocate and engage in community activities, and children champion physical activity and balanced screen time. Together, families educate about mental health, maintain a clean home, and advocate for health initiatives. Through these collective efforts, homizens evolve into Earthizens, contributing to a sustainable and harmonious world. This journey is a call to action for families to unite and create a better future for all.*

Goal 3: Good Health and Well-being

| Act | Measurement Metric | Frequency | Target |
| --- | --- | --- | --- |
| Exercise daily | Minutes of exercise | Daily | 30 minutes/day |
| Eat balanced meals | Number of balanced meals | Daily | 3 meals/day |
| Schedule health check-ups | Number of check-ups | Annually | 2 check-ups/year |
| Practice mindfulness | Minutes of mindfulness | Daily | 10 minutes/day |
| Ensure adequate sleep | Hours of sleep | Daily | 8 hours/night |
| Limit screen time | Hours of screen time | Daily | 2 hours/day |

| Act | Measurement Metric | Frequency | Target |
|---|---|---|---|
| Maintain a clean home | Number of cleaning sessions | Weekly | 2 sessions/week |
| Educate about mental health | Number of sessions | Monthly | 1 session/month |
| Avoid smoking and limit alcohol | Number of days without smoking/alcohol | Monthly | 25 days/month |
| Participate in health initiatives | Number of initiatives | Quarterly | 1 initiative/quarter |

### Goal 4: Quality Education

1. Read together as a family daily.
2. Encourage lifelong learning through online courses.
3. Support local schools with donations or volunteering.
4. Create a dedicated study space at home.
5. Discuss current events to enhance critical thinking.
6. Encourage creative activities like arts and crafts.
7. Promote digital literacy.
8. Participate in educational community events.
9. Teach practical life skills.
10. Advocate for inclusive education policies.

The journey from homizen to earthizen involves each family member playing a crucial role in embracing Sustainable Development Goal 4: Quality Education. This transformation is about fostering a collective mindset that prioritizes lifelong learning, inclusivity, and the development of essential skills. By engaging in specific acts, families can significantly contribute to promoting quality education, ultimately becoming proactive Earthizens.

Elders: Elders in the family can lead by example in advocating for inclusive education and teaching life skills. They can initiate quarterly advocacy actions, such as writing letters to local representatives or participating in community meetings to promote policies that support inclusive education. Additionally, elders can teach life skills to younger family members, offering guidance on practical skills such as cooking, budgeting, and time management. Their wisdom and experience can provide valuable insights and encouragement, helping younger family members build confidence and resilience. Elders can also discuss current events with the *family through weekly sessions, sharing stories and insights that highlight the importance of staying informed and engaged with the world.*

*Parents: Parents are instrumental in promoting digital literacy and supporting local schools. They can actively participate in educational events by organizing family outings to local workshops or seminars that focus on digital literacy and technology. This quarterly activity of participating in at least one educational event can instill a sense of responsibility towards promoting quality education in children. Furthermore, parents can support local schools by making conscious choices about their donations and volunteer hours. This could include volunteering at school events or donating resources to support educational programs. Through these actions, parents demonstrate the importance of supporting education, guiding their family towards becoming responsible Earthizens.*

*Kids: Children, with their boundless energy and curiosity, can be champions of reading together and encouraging creative activities. They can participate in daily actions that promote reading, such as setting aside 30 minutes each day to read with family members. These activities help children understand and appreciate the importance of literacy and the joy of reading. Additionally, kids can encourage creative activities by participating in weekly sessions that involve arts and crafts, music, or other creative pursuits. These experiences teach children the value of creativity and instill a sense of responsibility towards fostering a love for learning.*

*Family Activities: As a cohesive unit, families can engage in activities that promote awareness about quality education and create study spaces. Monthly sessions where the family discusses the importance of creating dedicated study spaces and the impact of a conducive learning environment can be enlightening. These discussions, facilitated by parents or elders, can involve interactive activities like quizzes or debates to make learning engaging for kids. Supporting initiatives that promote quality education is another area where families can contribute collectively. Quarterly actions such as advocating for inclusive education or participating in educational events help raise awareness and promote lifelong learning within the community.*

*Collective Advocacy: Families can advocate for quality education by participating in campaigns that highlight the importance of promoting inclusive and equitable education for all. This could involve writing letters to local representatives or joining advocacy groups that work towards establishing and maintaining quality education policies. By engaging in these activities together, families reinforce the values of lifelong learning and inclusivity. Promoting awareness about quality education within the family, educating about digital literacy, and supporting local schools are foundational steps in this journey. Each family member, from elders to kids, contributes uniquely to these efforts, creating a ripple effect that extends beyond the household.*

*The Path to Earthizenship: The journey from homizen to earthizen is marked by a series of transformative actions that align with the Earthizens Revolution 2050. By reading together, families cultivate a culture of literacy and responsibility. Encouraging online courses and participating in educational events instills a deep sense of commitment to promoting lifelong learning. Advocating for inclusive education and educating about digital literacy empowers families to be active participants in their communities. Creating study spaces, discussing current events, and supporting local schools foster a sense of global Earthizenship and responsibility.*

*As families engage in these acts, they transition from being homizens—citizens of their homes—to Earthizens, proactive global citizens committed to quality education. This transformation is not just about individual actions but about fostering a collective mindset that aligns with global sustainability and lifelong learning. By embracing these practices, families contribute to promoting quality education, ultimately achieving the vision of a harmonious and sustainable world.*

*In conclusion, the journey from homizen to earthizen is a transformative process that involves every family member. Elders provide wisdom and guidance, parents advocate and engage in community activities, and children champion literacy and creativity. Together, families educate about quality education, create study spaces, and advocate for inclusive education. Through these collective efforts, homizens evolve into Earthizens, contributing to a sustainable and harmonious world. This journey is a call to action for families to unite and create a better future for all.*

Goal 4: Quality Education

| Act | Measurement Metric | Frequency | Target |
|---|---|---|---|
| Read together | Minutes of reading | Daily | 30 minutes/day |
| Encourage online courses | Number of courses completed | Quarterly | 1 course/quarter |
| Support local schools | Number of donations/volunteer hours | Monthly | 2 donations/5 hours |
| Create study space | Number of study sessions | Daily | 1 session/day |

| Act | Measurement Metric | Frequency | Target |
|---|---|---|---|
| Discuss current events | Number of discussions | Weekly | 2 discussions/week |
| Encourage creative activities | Number of activities | Weekly | 2 activities/week |
| Promote digital literacy | Number of sessions | Monthly | 1 session/month |
| Participate in educational events | Number of events | Quarterly | 1 event/quarter |
| Teach life skills | Number of skills taught | Monthly | 2 skills/month |
| Advocate for inclusive education | Number of advocacy actions | Quarterly | 1 action/quarter |

### Goal 5: Gender Equality

1. Share household chores equally.
2. Encourage all family members to pursue their interests.
3. Discuss gender equality openly.
4. Support women-owned businesses.
5. Challenge gender stereotypes in media.
6. Promote equal opportunities in education and sports.
7. Advocate for women's rights in the community.
8. Celebrate achievements of women and girls.
9. Provide mentorship to young girls.
10. Participate in gender equality campaigns.

The journey from homizen to earthizen involves each family member playing a crucial role in embracing Sustainable Development Goal 5: Gender Equality. This transformation is about fostering a collective mindset that prioritizes equality, inclusivity, and the empowerment of all genders. By engaging in specific acts, families can significantly contribute to promoting gender equality, ultimately becoming proactive Earthizens.

Elders: Elders in the family can lead by example in advocating for women's rights and providing mentorship. They can initiate quarterly advocacy actions, such as writing letters to local representatives or participating in community meetings to promote policies that support gender equality. Additionally, elders can mentor *younger family members or individuals in the community, offering guidance and support to help them navigate challenges and achieve their goals. Their wisdom and experience can provide valuable insights and encouragement, helping mentees build confidence and resilience. Elders can also discuss gender equality with the family through monthly sessions, sharing stories and insights that highlight the importance of equal opportunities and the impact of gender stereotypes.*

*Parents: Parents are instrumental in promoting equal opportunities and supporting women-owned businesses. They can actively participate in campaigns by organizing family outings to local events that focus on gender equality and women's empowerment. This annual activity of participating in at least two campaigns can instill a sense of responsibility towards promoting gender equality in children. Furthermore, parents can support women-owned businesses by making conscious choices about the products they purchase. This could include buying from businesses owned by women and educating the family about the impact of their purchasing decisions. Through these actions, parents demonstrate the importance of supporting gender equality, guiding their family towards becoming responsible Earthizens.*

*Kids: Children, with their boundless energy and curiosity, can be champions of sharing household chores and challenging stereotypes. They can participate in daily actions that promote equality at home, such as sharing household chores equally among all family members. These activities help children understand and appreciate the importance of equal responsibilities and the value of teamwork. Additionally, kids can challenge stereotypes by learning about gender equality and encouraging their peers to break down traditional gender roles. These experiences teach children the value of inclusivity and instill a sense of responsibility towards creating an equitable society.*

*Family Activities: As a cohesive unit, families can engage in activities that promote awareness about gender equality and celebrate achievements. Monthly sessions where the family discusses the importance of promoting equal opportunities and the impact of advocacy actions on gender equality can be enlightening. These discussions, facilitated by parents or elders, can involve interactive activities like quizzes or debates to make learning engaging for kids. Supporting initiatives that promote gender equality is another area where families can contribute collectively. Quarterly actions such as advocating for women's rights or participating in mentorship programs help raise awareness and promote inclusive practices within the community.*

*Collective Advocacy: Families can advocate for gender equality by participating in campaigns that highlight the importance of promoting equal opportunities and supporting women's empowerment. This could involve writing letters to local representatives or joining advocacy groups that work towards establishing and maintaining gender equality policies. By engaging in these activities together, families reinforce the values of inclusivity and equality. Promoting awareness about gender equality within the family, educating about equal opportunities, and supporting women-owned businesses are foundational steps in this journey. Each family member, from elders to kids, contributes uniquely to these efforts, creating a ripple effect that extends beyond the household.*

*The Path to Earthizenship: The journey from homizen to earthizen is marked by a series of transformative actions that align with the Earthizens Revolution 2050. By sharing household chores, families cultivate a culture of equality and responsibility. Encouraging interests and participating in campaigns instills a deep sense of commitment to promoting gender equality. Advocating for women's rights and educating about gender equality empowers families to be active participants in their communities. Supporting women-owned businesses, challenging stereotypes, and promoting equal opportunities foster a sense of global Earthizenship and responsibility.*

*As families engage in these acts, they transition from being homizens—citizens of their homes—to Earthizens, proactive global citizens committed to gender equality. This transformation is not just about individual actions but about fostering a collective mindset that aligns with global sustainability and equality. By embracing these practices, families contribute to promoting gender equality, ultimately achieving the vision of a harmonious and inclusive world.*

*In conclusion, the journey from homizen to earthizen is a transformative process that involves every family member. Elders provide wisdom and guidance, parents advocate and engage in community activities, and children champion equal responsibilities and inclusivity. Together, families educate about gender equality, support women-owned businesses, and advocate for women's rights. Through these collective efforts, homizens evolve into Earthizens, contributing to a sustainable and harmonious world. This journey is a call to action for families to unite and create a better future for all.*

Goal 5: Gender Equality

| Act | Measurement Metric | Frequency | Target |
| --- | --- | --- | --- |
| Share household chores | Number of chores shared | Daily | 3 chores/day |
| Encourage interests | Number of activities supported | Weekly | 2 activities/week |

| Act | Measurement Metric | Frequency | Target |
|---|---|---|---|
| Discuss gender equality | Number of discussions | Monthly | 1 discussion/month |
| Support women-owned businesses | Amount spent | Monthly | ₹500/month |
| Challenge stereotypes | Number of actions | Monthly | 2 actions/month |
| Promote equal opportunities | Number of opportunities | Quarterly | 2 opportunities/quarter |
| Advocate for women's rights | Number of advocacy actions | Quarterly | 1 action/quarter |
| Celebrate achievements | Number of celebrations | Monthly | 1 celebration/month |
| Provide mentorship | Number of mentees | Quarterly | 1 mentee/quarter |
| Participate in campaigns | Number of campaigns | Annually | 2 campaigns/year |

### Goal 6: Clean Water and Sanitation

1. Fix leaks promptly to conserve water.
2. Install water-saving fixtures.
3. Use eco-friendly cleaning products.
4. Collect rainwater for gardening.
5. Educate about the importance of water conservation.
6. Avoid single-use plastics.
7. Participate in local clean-up drives.
8. Advocate for clean water initiatives.
9. Reduce water usage in daily activities.
10. Support organizations working on water sanitation.

The journey from homizen to earthizen involves each family member playing a crucial role in embracing Sustainable Development Goal 6: Clean Water and Sanitation. This transformation is about fostering a collective mindset that prioritizes water conservation, sanitation, and sustainable practices. By engaging in specific acts, families can significantly contribute to promoting clean water and sanitation, ultimately becoming proactive Earthizens.

Elders: Elders in the family can lead by example in advocating for clean water and educating about water conservation. They can initiate quarterly advocacy actions, such as writing letters to local representatives or participating in community *meetings to promote policies that support clean water initiatives. Additionally, elders can educate the family about water conservation through monthly sessions, discussing the importance of preserving water resources and the impact of water usage on the environment. Their stories and insights can provide a rich context for understanding the significance of clean water and inspire younger family members to get involved.*

*Parents: Parents are instrumental in promoting water-saving practices and supporting water sanitation organizations. They can actively participate in clean-up drives by organizing family outings to local parks or neighborhoods. This quarterly activity of participating in at least one clean-up drive can instill a sense of responsibility towards promoting clean water in children. Furthermore, parents can support water sanitation organizations by making conscious choices about their donations. This could include donating to organizations that prioritize water sanitation and educating the family about the impact of their contributions. Through these actions, parents demonstrate the importance of supporting clean water initiatives, guiding their family towards becoming responsible Earthizens.*

*Kids: Children, with their boundless energy and curiosity, can be champions of reducing water usage and avoiding single-use plastics. They can participate in weekly actions that promote water conservation, such as turning off taps when not in use or using water-saving fixtures. These activities help children understand and appreciate the impact of their choices on water resources. Additionally, kids can avoid single-use plastics by learning about sustainable alternatives and encouraging their peers to make environmentally conscious choices. These experiences teach children the value of reducing waste and instill a sense of responsibility towards creating a sustainable society.*

*Family Activities: As a cohesive unit, families can engage in activities that promote awareness about clean water and collect rainwater. Monthly sessions where the family discusses the importance of using eco-friendly products and the impact of water choices on the environment can be enlightening. These discussions, facilitated by parents or elders, can involve interactive activities like quizzes or debates to make learning engaging for kids. Supporting initiatives that promote water conservation is another area where families can contribute collectively. Monthly actions such as installing water-saving fixtures or collecting rainwater help raise awareness and promote sustainable water practices within the community.*

*Collective Advocacy: Families can advocate for clean water by participating in campaigns that highlight the importance of promoting water conservation and sanitation. This could involve writing letters to local representatives or joining advocacy groups that work towards establishing and maintaining clean water policies. By engaging in these activities together, families reinforce the values of sustainability and environmental stewardship. Promoting awareness about clean water within the family, educating about water-saving practices, and supporting water sanitation organizations are foundational steps in this journey. Each family member, from elders to kids, contributes uniquely to these efforts, creating a ripple effect that extends beyond the household.*

*The Path to Earthizenship: The journey from homizen to earthizen is marked by a series of transformative actions that align with the Earthizens Revolution 2050. By fixing leaks and installing water-saving fixtures, families cultivate a culture of environmental stewardship and responsibility. Using eco-friendly products and participating in clean-up drives instills a deep sense of commitment to promoting clean water. Advocating for clean water policies and educating about water conservation empowers families to be active participants in their communities. Collecting rainwater, avoiding single-use plastics, and supporting water sanitation organizations foster a sense of global Earthizenship and responsibility.*

*As families engage in these acts, they transition from being homizens—citizens of their homes—to Earthizens, proactive global citizens committed to clean water and sanitation. This transformation is not just about individual actions but about fostering a collective mindset that aligns with global sustainability and water conservation. By embracing these practices, families contribute to promoting clean water and sanitation, ultimately achieving the vision of a harmonious and sustainable world.*

*In summary, the journey from homizen to earthizen is a transformative process that involves every family member. Elders provide wisdom and guidance, parents advocate and engage in community activities, and children champion sustainable practices and water conservation. Together, families educate about clean water, reduce water usage, and advocate for clean water policies. Through these collective efforts, homizens evolve into Earthizens, contributing to a sustainable and harmonious world. This journey is a call to action for families to unite and create a better future for all.*

Goal 6: Clean Water and Sanitation

| Act | Measurement Metric | Frequency | Target |
| --- | --- | --- | --- |
| Fix leaks | Number of leaks fixed | Monthly | 1 leak/month |
| Install water-saving fixtures | Number of fixtures installed | Quarterly | 1 fixture/quarter |

| Act | Measurement Metric | Frequency | Target |
|---|---|---|---|
| Use eco-friendly products | Number of products used | Monthly | 5 products/month |
| Collect rainwater | Liters of rainwater collected | Monthly | 100 liters/month |
| Educate about water conservation | Number of sessions | Monthly | 1 session/month |
| Avoid single-use plastics | Number of items avoided | Weekly | 5 items/week |
| Participate in clean-up drives | Number of drives | Quarterly | 1 drive/quarter |
| Advocate for clean water | Number of advocacy actions | Quarterly | 1 action/quarter |
| Reduce water usage | Liters of water saved | Monthly | 10% reduction/month |
| Support water sanitation organizations | Amount donated | Annually | ₹1000/year |

### Goal 7: Affordable and Clean Energy

1. Switch to energy-efficient appliances.
2. Use LED bulbs.
3. Install solar panels if possible.
4. Turn off lights and electronics when not in use.
5. Use public transport or carpool.
6. Educate about renewable energy sources.
7. Advocate for clean energy policies.
8. Participate in energy conservation programs.
9. Insulate your home to reduce heating and cooling needs.
10. Support green energy providers.

The journey from homizen to earthizen involves each family member playing a crucial role in embracing Sustainable Development Goal 7: Affordable and Clean Energy. This transformation is about fostering a collective mindset that prioritizes energy efficiency, renewable energy, and sustainable practices. By engaging in specific acts, families can significantly contribute to promoting affordable and clean energy, ultimately becoming proactive Earthizens.

*Elders:* Elders in the family can lead by example in advocating for clean energy policies and educating about renewable energy. They can initiate quarterly advocacy actions, such as writing letters to local representatives or participating in community meetings to promote policies that support clean energy. Additionally, elders can educate the family about renewable energy through monthly sessions, discussing the benefits of solar, wind, and other renewable energy sources. Their stories and insights can provide a rich context for understanding the significance of clean energy and inspire younger family members to get involved.

*Parents:* Parents are instrumental in promoting energy efficiency and supporting green energy providers. They can actively participate in conservation programs by organizing family outings to local events that focus on energy conservation and sustainability. This annual activity of participating in at least one conservation program can instill a sense of responsibility towards promoting clean energy in children. Furthermore, parents can support green energy providers by making conscious choices about their energy consumption. This could include investing in renewable energy sources for the home or supporting community renewable energy projects. Through these actions, parents demonstrate the importance of sustainable energy use, guiding their family towards becoming responsible Earthizens.

*Kids:* Children, with their boundless energy and curiosity, can be champions of reducing energy consumption and using public transportation. They can participate in weekly actions that promote energy reduction, such as turning off lights when not in use or using energy-efficient appliances. These activities help children understand and appreciate the impact of their choices on the environment. Additionally, kids can use public transportation or carpool by learning about the benefits of reducing car usage and encouraging their peers to make environmentally conscious choices. These experiences teach children the value of reducing their carbon footprint and instill a sense of responsibility towards creating a sustainable society.

*Family Activities:* As a cohesive unit, families can engage in activities that promote awareness about renewable energy and insulate their home. Monthly sessions where the family discusses the importance of using renewable energy sources and the impact of energy choices on the environment can be enlightening. These discussions, facilitated by parents or elders, can involve interactive activities like quizzes or debates to make learning engaging for kids. Supporting initiatives that promote energy efficiency is another area where families can contribute collectively.

*Annual actions such as installing solar panels or insulating the home help raise awareness and promote sustainable energy practices within the community.*

*Collective Advocacy: Families can advocate for clean energy policies by participating in campaigns that highlight the importance of promoting renewable energy. This could involve writing letters to local representatives or joining advocacy groups that work towards establishing and maintaining clean energy policies. By engaging in these activities together, families reinforce the values of sustainability and environmental stewardship. Promoting awareness about renewable energy within the family, educating about energy-efficient appliances, and supporting green energy providers are foundational steps in this journey. Each family member, from elders to kids, contributes uniquely to these efforts, creating a ripple effect that extends beyond the household.*

*The Path to Earthizenship: The journey from homizen to earthizen is marked by a series of transformative actions that align with the Earthizens Revolution 2050. By switching to energy-efficient appliances, families cultivate a culture of environmental stewardship and responsibility. Using LED bulbs and participating in conservation programs instills a deep sense of commitment to promoting clean energy. Advocating for clean energy policies and educating about renewable energy empowers families to be active participants in their communities. Turning off lights and electronics, using public transportation, and supporting green energy providers foster a sense of global Earthizenship and responsibility.*

*As families engage in these acts, they transition from being homizens—citizens of their homes—to Earthizens, proactive global citizens committed to affordable and clean energy. This transformation is not just about individual actions but about fostering a collective mindset that aligns with global sustainability and energy efficiency. By embracing these practices, families contribute to promoting affordable and clean energy, ultimately achieving the vision of a harmonious and sustainable world.*

*In conclusion, the journey from homizen to earthizen is a transformative process that involves every family member. Elders provide wisdom and guidance, parents advocate and engage in community activities, and children champion sustainable practices and energy conservation. Together, families educate about renewable energy, reduce energy consumption, and advocate for clean energy policies. Through these collective efforts, homizens evolve into Earthizens, contributing to a sustainable and harmonious world. This journey is a call to action for families to unite and create a better future for all.*

Goal 7: Affordable and Clean Energy

| Act | Measurement Metric | Frequency | Target |
| --- | --- | --- | --- |
| Switch to energy-efficient appliances | Number of appliances | Annually | 2 appliances/year |
| Use LED bulbs | Number of bulbs | Monthly | 5 bulbs/month |
| Install solar panels | Number of panels | Annually | 1 panel/year |
| Turn off lights/electronics | Hours of usage reduced | Daily | 2 hours/day |
| Use public transport/carpool | Number of trips | Weekly | 3 trips/week |
| Educate about renewable energy | Number of sessions | Monthly | 1 session/month |
| Advocate for clean energy policies | Number of advocacy actions | Quarterly | 1 action/quarter |
| Participate in conservation programs | Number of programs | Annually | 1 program/year |
| Insulate home | Amount of insulation added | Annually | 1 project/year |
| Support green energy providers | Amount spent | Monthly | ₹500/month |

### Goal 8: Decent Work and Economic Growth

1. Support fair trade products.
2. Encourage entrepreneurship within the family.
3. Promote work-life balance.
4. Advocate for fair wages and labor rights.
5. Participate in local economic development initiatives.
6. Educate about financial management.
7. Support local businesses.
8. Volunteer for job training programs.
9. Promote ethical consumerism.
10. Invest in sustainable businesses.

*The journey from homizen to earthizen involves each family member playing a crucial role in embracing Sustainable Development Goal 8: Decent Work and*

Economic Growth. This transformation is about fostering a collective mindset that prioritizes fair trade, entrepreneurship, work-life balance, and sustainable economic practices. By engaging in specific acts, families can significantly contribute to promoting decent work and economic growth, ultimately becoming proactive Earthizens.

Elders: Elders in the family can lead by example in advocating for fair wages and educating about financial management. They can initiate quarterly advocacy actions, such as writing letters to local representatives or participating in community meetings to promote policies that support fair wages. Additionally, elders can educate the family about financial management through monthly sessions, discussing the importance of budgeting, saving, and investing wisely. Their stories and insights can provide a rich context for understanding the significance of financial literacy and inspire younger family members to get involved.

Parents: Parents are instrumental in promoting work-life balance and supporting local businesses. They can actively participate in economic initiatives by organizing family outings to local events that focus on economic development and community support. This annual activity of participating in at least one economic initiative can instill a sense of responsibility towards promoting economic growth in children. Furthermore, parents can support local businesses by making conscious choices about the products they purchase. This could include buying from local shops and educating the family about the impact of their purchasing decisions. Through these actions, parents demonstrate the importance of supporting local economies, guiding their family towards becoming responsible Earthizens.

Kids: Children, with their boundless energy and curiosity, can be champions of promoting ethical consumerism and volunteering for job training. They can participate in monthly actions that promote ethical consumerism, such as organizing school events that highlight the importance of buying ethically produced goods or joining clubs that advocate for fair trade. These activities help children understand and appreciate the impact of their choices on global trade and sustainability. Additionally, kids can volunteer for job training by dedicating a few hours each quarter to activities like community service or charity events. These experiences teach children the value of working together for a common cause and instill a sense of responsibility towards creating a sustainable society.

Family Activities: As a cohesive unit, families can engage in activities that promote awareness about decent work and economic growth and invest in sustainable businesses. Monthly sessions where the family discusses the importance of supporting fair trade products and the impact of ethical consumerism on the economy can be enlightening. These discussions, facilitated by parents or elders, can involve interactive activities like quizzes or debates to make learning engaging for kids. Supporting initiatives that promote decent work is another area where families can contribute collectively. Quarterly actions such as advocating for fair wages or participating in job training programs help raise awareness and promote sustainable economic practices within the community.

Collective Advocacy: Families can advocate for decent work and economic growth by participating in campaigns that highlight the importance of promoting fair trade and supporting local businesses. This could involve writing letters to local representatives or joining advocacy groups that work towards establishing and maintaining fair economic practices. By engaging in these activities together, families reinforce the values of sustainability and economic growth. Promoting awareness about decent work within the family, educating about financial management, and supporting local businesses are foundational steps in this journey. Each family member, from elders to kids, contributes uniquely to these efforts, creating a ripple effect that extends beyond the household.

The Path to Earthizenship: The journey from homizen to earthizen is marked by a series of transformative actions that align with the Earthizens Revolution 2050. By supporting fair trade products, families cultivate a culture of ethical consumerism and responsibility. Encouraging entrepreneurship and participating in economic initiatives instills a deep sense of commitment to promoting economic growth. Advocating for fair wages and educating about financial management empowers families to be active participants in their communities. Promoting work-life balance, supporting local businesses, and investing in sustainable businesses foster a sense of global Earthizenship and responsibility.

As families engage in these acts, they transition from being homizens—citizens of their homes—to Earthizens, proactive global citizens committed to decent work and economic growth. This transformation is not just about individual actions but about fostering a collective mindset that aligns with global sustainability and economic development. By embracing these practices, families contribute to promoting decent work and economic growth, ultimately achieving the vision of a harmonious and sustainable world.

In summary, the journey from homizen to earthizen is a transformative process that involves every family member. Elders provide wisdom and guidance, parents advocate and engage in community activities, and children champion ethical consumerism and job training. Together, families educate about financial management, support local businesses, and advocate for fair wages. Through these collective efforts, homizens evolve into Earthizens, contributing to a sustainable and *harmonious world. This journey is a call to action for families to unite and create a better future for all.*

Goal 8: Decent Work and Economic Growth

| Act | Measurement Metric | Frequency | Target |
| --- | --- | --- | --- |
| Support fair trade products | Amount spent | Monthly | ₹500/month |
| Encourage entrepreneurship | Number of initiatives | Annually | 1 initiative/year |
| Promote work-life balance | Number of balanced days | Monthly | 20 days/month |
| Advocate for fair wages | Number of advocacy actions | Quarterly | 1 action/quarter |
| Participate in economic initiatives | Number of initiatives | Annually | 1 initiative/year |
| Educate about financial management | Number of sessions | Monthly | 1 session/month |
| Support local businesses | Amount spent | Monthly | ₹1000/month |
| Volunteer for job training | Number of hours | Quarterly | 5 hours/quarter |
| Promote ethical consumerism | Number of actions | Monthly | 2 actions/month |
| Invest in sustainable businesses | Amount invested | Annually | ₹5000/year |

### Goal 9: Industry, Innovation, and Infrastructure

1. *Support local tech startups.*
2. *Encourage STEM education.*
3. *Use public transportation.*
4. *Advocate for better infrastructure in the community.*
5. *Participate in innovation challenges.*
6. *Promote recycling and upcycling.*
7. *Support sustainable construction practices.*
8. *Educate about the importance of infrastructure.*
9. *Use digital tools to improve efficiency.*

*10. Invest in smart home technologies.*

*The journey from homizen to earthizen involves each family member playing a crucial role in embracing Sustainable Development Goal 9: Industry, Innovation, and Infrastructure. This transformation is about fostering a collective mindset that prioritizes technological advancement, sustainable practices, and robust infrastructure. By engaging in specific acts, families can significantly contribute to promoting industry, innovation, and infrastructure, ultimately becoming proactive Earthizens.*

*Elders: Elders in the family can lead by example in advocating for better infrastructure and supporting sustainable construction. They can initiate quarterly advocacy actions, such as writing letters to local representatives or participating in community meetings to promote policies that support infrastructure development. Additionally, elders can educate the family about the importance of infrastructure through monthly sessions, discussing how robust infrastructure contributes to economic growth and community well-being. Their stories and insights can provide a rich context for understanding the significance of infrastructure development and inspire younger family members to get involved.*

*Parents: Parents are instrumental in promoting sustainable practices and engaging in community projects. They can actively participate in innovation challenges by organizing family outings to local events that focus on technological advancements and creative solutions. This annual activity of participating in at least one innovation challenge can instill a sense of responsibility towards promoting innovation in children. Furthermore, parents can support local tech startups by making conscious choices about their investments. This could include investing in startups that prioritize eco-friendly practices and educating the family about the impact of their investment decisions. Through these actions, parents demonstrate the importance of supporting industry and innovation, guiding their family towards becoming responsible Earthizens.*

*Kids: Children, with their boundless energy and curiosity, can be champions of using public transportation and promoting recycling/upcycling. They can participate in weekly actions that promote the use of public transportation, such as taking the bus or cycling to school. These activities help children understand and appreciate the impact of their choices on urban environments. Additionally, kids can promote recycling/upcycling by learning about sustainable alternatives and encouraging their peers to make environmentally conscious choices. These experiences teach children the value of reducing waste and instill a sense of responsibility towards creating a sustainable society.*

*Family Activities: As a cohesive unit, families can engage in activities that promote awareness about infrastructure and use digital tools. Monthly sessions where the family discusses the importance of using digital tools to improve efficiency and the impact of technological choices on the environment can be enlightening. These discussions, facilitated by parents or elders, can involve interactive activities like quizzes or debates to make learning engaging for kids. Supporting initiatives that promote the use of digital tools is another area where families can contribute collectively. Monthly actions such as exploring new technologies or implementing smart home solutions help raise awareness and promote sustainable practices within the community.*

*Collective Advocacy: Families can advocate for better infrastructure by participating in campaigns that highlight the importance of developing robust infrastructure. This could involve writing letters to local representatives or joining advocacy groups that work towards establishing and maintaining infrastructure projects. By engaging in these activities together, families reinforce the values of sustainability and technological advancement. Promoting awareness about infrastructure within the family, educating about STEM education, and supporting local tech startups are foundational steps in this journey. Each family member, from elders to kids, contributes uniquely to these efforts, creating a ripple effect that extends beyond the household.*

*The Path to Earthizenship: The journey from homizen to earthizen is marked by a series of transformative actions that align with the Earthizens Revolution 2050. By supporting local tech startups, families cultivate a culture of innovation and responsibility. Encouraging STEM education and participating in innovation challenges instills a deep sense of commitment to promoting technological advancements. Advocating for better infrastructure and educating about infrastructure empowers families to be active participants in their communities. Using public transportation, promoting recycling/upcycling, and supporting sustainable construction foster a sense of global Earthizenship and responsibility.*

*As families engage in these acts, they transition from being homizens—citizens of their homes—to Earthizens, proactive global citizens committed to industry, innovation, and infrastructure. This transformation is not just about individual actions but about fostering a collective mindset that aligns with global sustainability and technological advancement. By embracing these practices, families contribute to promoting industry, innovation, and infrastructure, ultimately achieving the vision of a harmonious and sustainable world.*

*In summary, the journey from homizen to earthizen is a transformative process that involves every family member. Elders provide wisdom and guidance, parents advocate and engage in community activities, and children champion sustainable practices and technological advancements. Together, families educate about infrastructure, use public transportation, and advocate for better infrastructure. Through these collective efforts, homizens evolve into Earthizens, contributing to a sustainable and harmonious world. This journey is a call to action for families to unite and create a better future for all.*

Goal 9: Industry, Innovation, and Infrastructure

| Act | Measurement Metric | Frequency | Target |
|---|---|---|---|
| Support local tech startups | Amount invested | Annually | ₹5000/year |
| Encourage STEM education | Number of sessions | Monthly | 1 session/month |
| Use public transportation | Number of trips | Weekly | 3 trips/week |
| Advocate for better infrastructure | Number of advocacy actions | Quarterly | 1 action/quarter |
| Participate in innovation challenges | Number of challenges | Annually | 1 challenge/year |
| Promote recycling/upcycling | Number of items recycled/upcycled | Monthly | 10 items/month |
| Support sustainable construction | Number of projects | Annually | 1 project/year |
| Educate about infrastructure | Number of sessions | Monthly | 1 session/month |
| Use digital tools | Number of tools used | Monthly | 2 tools/month |
| Invest in smart home tech | Amount invested | Annually | ₹5000/year |

### *Goal 10: Reduced Inequalities*

*1. Support policies that promote social inclusion.*
*2. Volunteer with organizations that help marginalized groups.*
*3. Educate about diversity and inclusion.*
*4. Advocate for equal opportunities.*

*5. Support businesses that promote diversity.*
*6. Participate in community dialogues on inequality.*
*7. Promote inclusive practices at home.*
*8. Mentor individuals from underrepresented groups.*
*9. Donate to causes that fight inequality.*
*10. Celebrate cultural diversity.*

*The journey from homizen to earthizen involves each family member playing a crucial role in embracing Sustainable Development Goal 10: Reduced Inequalities. This transformation is about fostering a collective mindset that prioritizes inclusivity, diversity, and equal opportunities. By engaging in specific acts, families can significantly contribute to reducing inequalities, ultimately becoming proactive Earthizens.*

*Elders: Elders in the family can lead by example in advocating for inclusive policies and mentoring underrepresented individuals. They can initiate quarterly advocacy actions, such as writing letters to local representatives or participating in community meetings to promote policies that support inclusivity. Additionally, elders can mentor underrepresented individuals by offering guidance and support to those who may not have access to such resources. Their wisdom and experience can provide valuable insights and encouragement, helping mentees navigate challenges and achieve their goals. Elders can also educate the family about diversity through monthly sessions, discussing the importance of embracing different cultures and backgrounds. Their stories and insights can provide a rich context for understanding the significance of inclusivity and inspire younger family members to get involved.*

*Parents: Parents are instrumental in promoting inclusive practices and engaging in community dialogues. They can actively participate in community dialogues by organizing family outings to local events that focus on inclusivity and diversity. This quarterly activity of participating in at least one community dialogue can instill a sense of responsibility towards promoting equality in children. Furthermore, parents can support diverse businesses by making conscious choices about the products they purchase. This could include buying from businesses owned by marginalized groups and educating the family about the impact of their purchasing decisions. Through these actions, parents demonstrate the importance of supporting diversity, guiding their family towards becoming responsible Earthizens.*

*Kids: Children, with their boundless energy and curiosity, can be champions of volunteering with marginalized groups and promoting inclusive practices. They can participate in monthly actions that promote inclusivity, such as organizing school events that celebrate different cultures or joining clubs that advocate for diversity.*

These activities help children understand and appreciate the richness of cultural diversity and the importance of equal opportunities. Additionally, kids can volunteer with marginalized groups by dedicating a few hours each month to activities like community service or charity events. These experiences teach children the value of working together for a common cause and instill a sense of responsibility towards creating an inclusive society.

Family Activities: As a cohesive unit, families can engage in activities that promote awareness about diversity and advocate for equal opportunities. Monthly sessions where the family discusses the importance of supporting inclusive policies and the impact of advocacy actions on reducing inequalities can be enlightening. These discussions, facilitated by parents or elders, can involve interactive activities like quizzes or debates to make learning engaging for kids. Supporting initiatives that promote equal opportunities is another area where families can contribute collectively. Quarterly actions such as participating in advocacy campaigns or supporting organizations that work towards equality help raise awareness and promote inclusive practices within the community.

Collective Advocacy: Families can advocate for inclusive policies by participating in campaigns that highlight the importance of promoting equality. This could involve writing letters to local representatives or joining advocacy groups that work towards establishing and maintaining inclusive policies. By engaging in these activities together, families reinforce the values of inclusivity and diversity. Promoting awareness about diversity within the family, educating about equal opportunities, and supporting diverse businesses are foundational steps in this journey. Each family member, from elders to kids, contributes uniquely to these efforts, creating a ripple effect that extends beyond the household.

The Path to Earthizenship: The journey from homizen to earthizen is marked by a series of transformative actions that align with the Earthizens Revolution 2050. By supporting inclusive policies, families cultivate a culture of equality and responsibility. Volunteering with marginalized groups and participating in community dialogues instills a deep sense of commitment to promoting inclusivity. Advocating for equal opportunities and educating about diversity empowers families to be active participants in their communities. Supporting diverse businesses, promoting inclusive practices, and mentoring underrepresented individuals foster a sense of global Earthizenship and responsibility.

As families engage in these acts, they transition from being homizens—citizens of their homes—to Earthizens, proactive global citizens committed to inclusivity and equality. This transformation is not just about individual actions but about fostering a collective mindset that aligns with global sustainability and equality. By embracing *these practices, families contribute to reducing inequalities, ultimately achieving the vision of a harmonious and inclusive world.*

*In summary, the journey from homizen to earthizen is a transformative process that involves every family member. Elders provide wisdom and guidance, parents advocate and engage in community activities, and children champion inclusive practices and diversity. Together, families educate about equal opportunities, volunteer with marginalized groups, and advocate for inclusive policies. Through these collective efforts, homizens evolve into Earthizens, contributing to a sustainable and harmonious world. This journey is a call to action for families to unite and create a better future for all.*

Goal 10: Reduced Inequalities

| Act | Measurement Metric | Frequency | Target |
| --- | --- | --- | --- |
| Support inclusive policies | Number of advocacy actions | Quarterly | 1 action/quarter |
| Volunteer with marginalized groups | Number of hours | Monthly | 5 hours/month |
| Educate about diversity | Number of sessions | Monthly | 1 session/month |
| Advocate for equal opportunities | Number of advocacy actions | Quarterly | 1 action/quarter |
| Support diverse businesses | Amount spent | Monthly | ₹500/month |
| Participate in community dialogues | Number of dialogues | Quarterly | 1 dialogue/quarter |
| Promote inclusive practices | Number of actions | Monthly | 2 actions/month |
| Mentor underrepresented individuals | Number of mentees | Quarterly | 1 mentee/ |

### Goal 11: Sustainable Cities and Communities

*1. Participate in local planning meetings.*
*2. Support public transportation.*
*3. Advocate for green spaces.*
*4. Reduce car usage.*
*5. Promote community gardens.*

6. *Participate in local clean-up events.*
7. *Support affordable housing initiatives.*
8. *Educate about sustainable living.*
9. *Use eco-friendly building materials.*
10. *Advocate for disaster-resilient infrastructure.*

*The journey from homizen to earthizen involves each family member playing a crucial role in embracing Sustainable Development Goal 11: Sustainable Cities and Communities. This transformation is about fostering a collective mindset that prioritizes the development of resilient, inclusive, and sustainable urban environments. By engaging in specific acts, families can significantly contribute to creating sustainable cities and communities, ultimately becoming proactive Earthizens.*

*Elders: Elders in the family can lead by example in advocating for disaster-resilient infrastructure and promoting community gardens. They can initiate quarterly advocacy actions, such as writing letters to local representatives or participating in community meetings to promote policies that support resilient infrastructure. Additionally, elders can educate the family about sustainable living through monthly sessions, discussing the importance of building resilient communities and the role each individual plays in achieving this goal. Their stories and insights can provide a rich context for understanding the significance of sustainable urban development and inspire younger family members to get involved.*

*Parents: Parents are instrumental in promoting sustainable practices and engaging in community projects. They can actively participate in clean-up events by organizing family outings to local parks or neighborhoods. This quarterly activity of participating in at least one clean-up event can instill a sense of responsibility towards the environment in children. Furthermore, parents can support affordable housing by making conscious choices about the initiatives they support. This could include volunteering for organizations that work towards providing affordable housing or advocating for policies that promote housing equity. Through these actions, parents demonstrate the importance of inclusive urban development, guiding their family towards becoming responsible Earthizens.*

*Kids: Children, with their boundless energy and curiosity, can be champions of reducing car usage and supporting public transportation. They can participate in weekly actions that promote car-free days, such as walking or cycling to school or using public transportation for family outings. These activities help children understand and appreciate the impact of their choices on urban environments. Additionally, kids can advocate for green spaces by learning about the benefits of parks and gardens and encouraging their peers to support local green initiatives.*

*These experiences teach children the value of creating sustainable cities and instill a sense of responsibility towards developing inclusive communities.*

*Family Activities: As a cohesive unit, families can engage in activities that promote awareness about sustainable living and use eco-friendly building materials. Monthly sessions where the family discusses the importance of using eco-friendly materials in construction and the impact of building choices on the environment can be enlightening. These discussions, facilitated by parents or elders, can involve interactive activities like quizzes or debates to make learning engaging for kids. Supporting initiatives that promote sustainable living is another area where families can contribute collectively. Monthly actions such as attending workshops on sustainable practices or implementing eco-friendly solutions at home help raise awareness and promote sustainable urban development within the community.*

*Collective Advocacy: Families can advocate for green spaces by participating in campaigns that highlight the importance of preserving and creating urban parks and gardens. This could involve writing letters to local representatives or joining advocacy groups that work towards establishing and maintaining green spaces. By engaging in these activities together, families reinforce the values of sustainability and environmental stewardship. Promoting awareness about sustainable living within the family, educating about eco-friendly building materials, and supporting affordable housing initiatives are foundational steps in this journey. Each family member, from elders to kids, contributes uniquely to these efforts, creating a ripple effect that extends beyond the household.*

*The Path to Earthizenship: The journey from homizen to earthizen is marked by a series of transformative actions that align with the Earthizens Revolution 2050. By participating in local planning meetings, families cultivate a culture of civic engagement and responsibility. Supporting public transportation and reducing car usage instills a deep sense of commitment to creating sustainable urban environments. Advocating for green spaces and promoting community gardens empowers families to be active participants in their communities. Participating in clean-up events, supporting affordable housing, and using eco-friendly building materials foster a sense of global Earthizenship and responsibility.*

*As families engage in these acts, they transition from being homizens—citizens of their homes—to Earthizens, proactive global citizens committed to sustainability and urban development. This transformation is not just about individual actions but about fostering a collective mindset that aligns with global sustainability and resilience. By embracing these practices, families contribute to creating sustainable cities and communities, ultimately achieving the vision of a harmonious and sustainable world.*

*In summary, the journey from homizen to earthizen is a transformative process that involves every family member. Elders provide wisdom and guidance, parents advocate and engage in community activities, and children champion sustainable practices and urban development. Together, families educate about sustainable living, reduce car usage, and advocate for green spaces. Through these collective efforts, homizens evolve into Earthizens, contributing to a sustainable and harmonious world. This journey is a call to action for families to unite and create a better future for all.*

Goal 11: Sustainable Cities and Communities

| Act | Measurement Metric | Frequency | Target |
|---|---|---|---|
| Participate in local planning meetings | Number of meetings attended | Quarterly | 1 meeting/quarter |
| Support public transportation | Number of trips | Weekly | 3 trips/week |
| Advocate for green spaces | Number of advocacy actions | Quarterly | 1 action/quarter |
| Reduce car usage | Number of car-free days | Monthly | 10 days/month |
| Promote community gardens | Number of gardens supported | Annually | 1 garden/year |
| Participate in clean-up events | Number of events | Quarterly | 1 event/quarter |
| Support affordable housing | Number of initiatives supported | Annually | 1 initiative/year |
| Educate about sustainable living | Number of sessions | Monthly | 1 session/month |
| Use eco-friendly building materials | Number of projects | Annually | 1 project/year |
| Advocate for disaster-resilient infrastructure | Number of advocacy actions | Quarterly | 1 action/quarter |

### Goal 12: Responsible Consumption and Production

1. Reduce, reuse, and recycle.
2. Buy second-hand items.
3. Avoid single-use plastics.
4. Support sustainable brands.
5. Plan meals to reduce food waste.
6. Compost organic waste.
7. Educate about sustainable consumption.
8. Participate in swap events.
9. Repair items instead of replacing them.
10. Advocate for sustainable production practices.

The journey from homizen to earthizen involves each family member playing a crucial role in embracing Sustainable Development Goal 12: Responsible Consumption and Production. This transformation is about fostering a collective mindset that prioritizes sustainable practices and mindful consumption. By engaging in specific acts, families can significantly contribute to reducing waste and promoting sustainable production, ultimately becoming proactive Earthizens.

Elders: Elders in the family can lead by example in advocating for sustainable production and educating about sustainable consumption. They can initiate quarterly advocacy actions, such as writing letters to local representatives or participating in community meetings to promote policies that support sustainable production. Additionally, elders can educate the family about sustainable consumption through monthly sessions, discussing the importance of reducing waste and making mindful choices. Their stories and insights can provide a rich context for understanding the significance of responsible consumption and inspire younger family members to get involved.

Parents: Parents are instrumental in promoting sustainable practices and engaging in community projects. They can actively participate in swap events by organizing family outings to local swap meets. This quarterly activity of participating in at least one swap event can instill a sense of responsibility towards the environment in children. Furthermore, parents can support sustainable brands by making conscious choices about the products they purchase. This could include buying from brands that prioritize eco-friendly practices and educating the family about the impact of their purchasing decisions. Through these actions, parents demonstrate the importance of supporting sustainable production, guiding their family towards becoming responsible Earthizens.

Kids: Children, with their boundless energy and curiosity, can be champions of reducing, reusing, and recycling. They can participate in weekly actions that *promote waste reduction, such as using reusable containers for school lunches or organizing recycling drives at school. These activities help children understand and appreciate the impact of their choices on the environment. Additionally, kids can avoid single-use plastics by learning about sustainable alternatives and encouraging their peers to make environmentally conscious choices. These experiences teach children the value of reducing waste and instill a sense of responsibility towards creating a sustainable society.*

*Family Activities: As a cohesive unit, families can engage in activities that promote awareness about responsible consumption and reduce food waste. Monthly sessions where the family discusses the importance of planning meals to reduce food waste and the impact of dietary choices on the environment can be enlightening. These discussions, facilitated by parents or elders, can involve interactive activities like quizzes or debates to make learning engaging for kids. Supporting initiatives that reduce food waste is another area where families can contribute collectively. Weekly actions such as planning meals to minimize leftovers or composting organic waste help raise awareness and promote sustainable dietary practices within the community.*

*Collective Advocacy: Families can advocate for sustainable production by participating in campaigns that highlight the importance of responsible consumption. This could involve writing letters to local representatives or joining advocacy groups that work towards promoting sustainable production practices. By engaging in these activities together, families reinforce the values of sustainability and environmental stewardship. Promoting awareness about responsible consumption within the family, educating about sustainable brands, and supporting initiatives that reduce waste are foundational steps in this journey. Each family member, from elders to kids, contributes uniquely to these efforts, creating a ripple effect that extends beyond the household.*

*The Path to Earthizenship: The journey from homizen to earthizen is marked by a series of transformative actions that align with the Earthizens Revolution 2050. By reducing, reusing, and recycling, families cultivate a culture of environmental stewardship and responsibility. Supporting sustainable brands and participating in swap events instills a deep sense of commitment to promoting sustainable production. Advocating for sustainable production and educating about responsible consumption empowers families to be active participants in their communities. Avoiding single-use plastics, planning meals to reduce food waste, and composting organic waste foster a sense of global Earthizenship and responsibility.*

*As families engage in these acts, they transition from being homizens—citizens of their homes—to Earthizens, proactive global citizens committed to sustainability and responsible consumption. This transformation is not just about individual actions but about fostering a collective mindset that aligns with global sustainability and conservation. By embracing these practices, families contribute to reducing waste and promoting sustainable production, ultimately achieving the vision of a harmonious and sustainable world.*

*In summary, the journey from homizen to earthizen is a transformative process that involves every family member. Elders provide wisdom and guidance, parents advocate and engage in community activities, and children champion sustainable practices and waste reduction. Together, families educate about responsible consumption, reduce food waste, and advocate for sustainable production. Through these collective efforts, homizens evolve into Earthizens, contributing to a sustainable and harmonious world. This journey is a call to action for families to unite and create a better future for all.*

Goal 12: Responsible Consumption and Production

| Act | Measurement Metric | Frequency | Target |
| --- | --- | --- | --- |
| Reduce, reuse, and recycle | Amount of waste reduced | Monthly | 10% reduction/month |
| Buy second-hand items | Number of items bought | Monthly | 2 items/month |
| Avoid single-use plastics | Number of items avoided | Weekly | 5 items/week |
| Support sustainable brands | Amount spent | Monthly | ₹500/month |
| Plan meals to reduce food waste | Amount of food waste reduced | Weekly | 20% reduction/week |
| Compost organic waste | Amount of compost produced | Monthly | 5 kg/month |
| Educate about sustainable consumption | Number of sessions | Monthly | 1 session/month |
| Participate in swap events | Number of events | Quarterly | 1 event/quarter |
| Repair items instead of replacing | Number of items repaired | Monthly | 2 items/month |

| Act | Measurement Metric | Frequency | Target |
|---|---|---|---|
| Advocate for sustainable production | Number of advocacy actions | Quarterly | 1 action/quarter |

### Goal 13: Climate Action

1. Reduce energy consumption.
2. Use public transport or cycle.
3. Plant trees.
4. Educate about climate change.
5. Support renewable energy.
6. Reduce meat consumption.
7. Participate in climate action campaigns.
8. Advocate for climate-friendly policies.
9. Use eco-friendly products.
10. Support conservation projects.

Embarking on the journey from homizen to earthizen involves each family member playing a crucial role in embracing Sustainable Development Goal 13: Climate Action. This transformation is about fostering a collective mindset that prioritizes the reduction of carbon footprints and the promotion of sustainable practices. By engaging in specific acts, families can significantly contribute to combating climate change, ultimately becoming proactive Earthizens.

Elders: Elders in the family can lead by example in advocating for climate-friendly policies and supporting conservation projects. They can initiate quarterly advocacy actions, such as writing letters to local representatives or participating in community meetings to promote policies that address climate change. Additionally, elders can educate the family about climate change through monthly sessions, discussing the science behind climate change and the importance of taking action. Their stories and insights can provide a rich context for understanding the significance of climate action and inspire younger family members to get involved.

Parents: Parents are instrumental in promoting sustainable practices and engaging in community projects. They can actively participate in climate action campaigns by organizing family outings to local events. This annual activity of participating in at least two climate action campaigns can instill a sense of responsibility towards the environment in children. Furthermore, parents can support renewable energy by making conscious choices about their energy consumption. This could include investing in renewable energy sources for the home or supporting community renewable energy projects. Through these actions, parents demonstrate the importance of sustainable energy use, guiding their family towards becoming responsible Earthizens.

Kids: Children, with their boundless energy and curiosity, can be champions of reducing energy consumption and using eco-friendly products. They can participate in weekly actions that promote energy reduction, such as turning off lights when not in use or using energy-efficient appliances. These activities help children understand and appreciate the impact of their choices on the environment. Additionally, kids can use eco-friendly products by learning about sustainable alternatives and encouraging their peers to make environmentally conscious choices. These experiences teach children the value of reducing their carbon footprint and instill a sense of responsibility towards creating a sustainable society.

Family Activities: As a cohesive unit, families can engage in activities that promote awareness about climate change and reduce meat consumption. Monthly sessions where the family discusses the importance of reducing meat consumption and the impact of dietary choices on the environment can be enlightening. These discussions, facilitated by parents or elders, can involve interactive activities like quizzes or debates to make learning engaging for kids. Supporting initiatives that reduce meat consumption is another area where families can contribute collectively. Weekly actions such as having meat-free days or exploring plant-based recipes help raise awareness and promote sustainable dietary practices within the community.

Collective Advocacy: Families can advocate for climate action by participating in campaigns that highlight the importance of reducing carbon footprints. This could involve writing letters to local representatives or joining advocacy groups that work towards promoting climate-friendly policies. By engaging in these activities together, families reinforce the values of sustainability and environmental stewardship. Promoting awareness about climate change within the family, educating about renewable energy, and supporting conservation projects are foundational steps in this journey. Each family member, from elders to kids, contributes uniquely to these efforts, creating a ripple effect that extends beyond the household.

The Path to Earthizenship: The journey from homizen to earthizen is marked by a series of transformative actions that align with the Earthizens Revolution 2050. By reducing energy consumption, families cultivate a culture of environmental stewardship and responsibility. Supporting renewable energy and participating in climate action campaigns instills a deep sense of commitment to combating climate change. Advocating for climate-friendly policies and educating about climate change empowers families to be active participants in their communities.

*Using eco-friendly products, reducing meat consumption, and supporting conservation projects foster a sense of global Earthizenship and responsibility.*

*As families engage in these acts, they transition from being homizens—citizens of their homes—to Earthizens, proactive global citizens committed to sustainability and climate action. This transformation is not just about individual actions but about fostering a collective mindset that aligns with global sustainability and conservation. By embracing these practices, families contribute to combating climate change, ultimately achieving the vision of a harmonious and sustainable world.*

*In conclusion, the journey from homizen to earthizen is a transformative process that involves every family member. Elders provide wisdom and guidance, parents advocate and engage in community activities, and children champion sustainable practices and energy conservation. Together, families educate about climate change, reduce energy consumption, and advocate for climate-friendly policies. Through these collective efforts, homizens evolve into Earthizens, contributing to a sustainable and harmonious world. This journey is a call to action for families to unite and create a better future for all.*

Goal 13: Climate Action

| Act | Measurement Metric | Frequency | Target |
|---|---|---|---|
| Reduce energy consumption | Amount of energy saved | Monthly | 10% reduction/month |
| Use public transport or cycle | Number of trips | Weekly | 3 trips/week |
| Plant trees | Number of trees planted | Annually | 5 trees/year |
| Educate about climate change | Number of sessions | Monthly | 1 session/month |
| Support renewable energy | Amount spent | Monthly | ₹500/month |
| Reduce meat consumption | Number of meat-free days | Weekly | 3 days/week |
| Participate in climate action campaigns | Number of campaigns | Annually | 2 campaigns/year |

| Act | Measurement Metric | Frequency | Target |
|---|---|---|---|
| Advocate for climate-friendly policies | Number of advocacy actions | Quarterly | 1 action/quarter |
| Use eco-friendly products | Number of products used | Monthly | 5 products/month |
| Support conservation projects | Number of projects supported | Annually | 1 project/year |

### Goal 14: Life Below Water

1. Reduce plastic use to prevent ocean pollution.
2. Support sustainable seafood.
3. Participate in beach clean-ups.
4. Educate about marine conservation.
5. Avoid products that harm marine life.
6. Advocate for marine protected areas.
7. Reduce water pollution.
8. Support organizations working on ocean conservation.
9. Use biodegradable products.
10. Promote awareness about the importance of oceans.

The journey from homizen to earthizen involves each family member playing a crucial role in embracing Sustainable Development Goal 14: Life Below Water. This transformation is about fostering a collective mindset that prioritizes the conservation and sustainable use of marine resources. By engaging in specific acts, families can significantly contribute to protecting and restoring life below water, ultimately becoming proactive Earthizens.

Elders: Elders in the family can lead by example in supporting ocean conservation organizations and advocating for marine protected areas. They can initiate annual donations to local or global ocean conservation organizations, sharing their knowledge and resources to support various initiatives. For instance, grandparents can participate in advocacy actions, helping to establish and maintain marine protected areas. Additionally, elders can educate the family about marine conservation through monthly sessions, discussing the importance of preserving marine ecosystems and the role each species plays in maintaining ecological balance. Their stories and insights can provide a rich context for understanding the significance of marine conservation.

*Parents:* Parents are instrumental in promoting sustainable practices and engaging in community projects. They can actively participate in beach clean-ups by organizing family outings to local beaches. This quarterly activity of participating in at least one beach clean-up can instill a sense of responsibility towards the environment in children. Furthermore, parents can support sustainable seafood by making conscious choices about the seafood they purchase and consume. This could include buying from certified sustainable sources and educating the family about the impact of overfishing. Through these actions, parents demonstrate the importance of sustainable marine resource use, guiding their family towards becoming responsible Earthizens.

*Kids:* Children, with their boundless energy and curiosity, can be champions of reducing plastic use and avoiding products that harm marine life. They can participate in weekly actions that promote plastic reduction, such as using reusable water bottles and bags or organizing school campaigns to reduce plastic waste. These activities help children understand and appreciate the impact of their choices on marine environments. Additionally, kids can avoid products that harm marine life by learning about eco-friendly alternatives and encouraging their peers to make sustainable choices. These experiences teach children the value of protecting marine life and instill a sense of responsibility towards creating a sustainable society.

*Family Activities:* As a cohesive unit, families can engage in activities that promote awareness about oceans and reduce water pollution. Monthly sessions where the family discusses the importance of protecting oceans and the impact of pollutants on marine life can be enlightening. These discussions, facilitated by parents or elders, can involve interactive activities like quizzes or debates to make learning engaging for kids. Supporting initiatives that reduce water pollution is another area where families can contribute collectively. Monthly actions such as using biodegradable products or supporting local water conservation efforts help raise awareness and promote sustainable practices within the community.

*Collective Advocacy:* Families can advocate for marine protected areas by participating in campaigns that highlight the importance of conserving marine habitats. This could involve writing letters to local representatives or joining advocacy groups that work towards establishing and maintaining marine protected areas. By engaging in these activities together, families reinforce the values of conservation and sustainability. Promoting awareness about oceans within the family, educating about marine conservation, and supporting ocean conservation organizations are foundational steps in this journey. Each family member, from elders to kids, contributes uniquely to these efforts, creating a ripple effect that extends beyond the household.

*The Path to Earthizenship: The journey from homizen to earthizen is marked by a series of transformative actions that align with the Earthizens Revolution 2050. By reducing plastic use, families cultivate a culture of environmental stewardship and responsibility. Supporting sustainable seafood and participating in beach clean-ups instills a deep sense of commitment to preserving marine ecosystems. Advocating for marine protected areas and educating about marine conservation empowers families to be active participants in their communities. Reducing water pollution, avoiding products that harm marine life, and supporting ocean conservation organizations foster a sense of global Earthizenship and responsibility.*

*As families engage in these acts, they transition from being homizens—citizens of their homes—to Earthizens, proactive global citizens committed to sustainability and conservation. This transformation is not just about individual actions but about fostering a collective mindset that aligns with global sustainability and conservation. By embracing these practices, families contribute to protecting and restoring life below water, ultimately achieving the vision of a harmonious and sustainable world.*

*In summary, the journey from homizen to earthizen is a transformative process that involves every family member. Elders provide wisdom and guidance, parents advocate and engage in community activities, and children champion sustainable practices and marine protection. Together, families educate about marine conservation, reduce water pollution, and advocate for marine protected areas. Through these collective efforts, homizens evolve into Earthizens, contributing to a sustainable and harmonious world. This journey is a call to action for families to unite and create a better future for all.*

Goal 14: Life Below Water

| Act | Measurement Metric | Frequency | Target |
|---|---|---|---|
| Reduce plastic use | Number of plastic items avoided | Weekly | 5 items/week |
| Support sustainable seafood | Amount spent | Monthly | ₹500/month |
| Participate in beach clean-ups | Number of clean-ups | Quarterly | 1 clean-up/quarter |
| Educate about marine conservation | Number of sessions | Monthly | 1 session/month |

| Act | Measurement Metric | Frequency | Target |
| --- | --- | --- | --- |
| Avoid products that harm marine life | Number of products avoided | Monthly | 5 products/month |
| Advocate for marine protected areas | Number of advocacy actions | Quarterly | 1 action/quarter |
| Reduce water pollution | Amount of pollutants reduced | Monthly | 10% reduction/month |
| Support ocean conservation organizations | Amount donated | Annually | ₹1000/year |
| Use biodegradable products | Number of products used | Monthly | 5 products/month |
| Promote awareness about oceans | Number of awareness actions | Quarterly | 1 action/quarter |

### Goal 15: Life on Land

1. Plant native trees and plants.
2. Support wildlife conservation efforts.
3. Reduce paper usage.
4. Educate about biodiversity.
5. Avoid products that harm wildlife.
6. Participate in reforestation projects.
7. Advocate for protected natural areas.
8. Reduce pesticide use.
9. Support sustainable agriculture.
10. Promote awareness about endangered species.

The journey from homizen to earthizen involves each family member playing a crucial role in embracing Sustainable Development Goal 15: Life on Land. This transformation is about fostering a collective mindset that prioritizes the conservation and sustainable use of terrestrial ecosystems. By engaging in specific acts, families can significantly contribute to protecting and restoring life on land, ultimately becoming proactive Earthizens.

*Elders: Elders in the family can lead by example in supporting wildlife conservation and advocating for protected areas. They can initiate annual collaborations with local wildlife conservation organizations, sharing their knowledge and resources to support various initiatives. For instance, grandparents can participate in wildlife conservation projects, helping to protect endangered species and their habitats. Additionally, elders can educate the family about biodiversity through monthly sessions, discussing the importance of preserving diverse ecosystems and the role each species plays in maintaining ecological balance. Their stories and insights can provide a rich context for understanding the significance of biodiversity conservation.*

*Parents: Parents are instrumental in promoting sustainable practices and engaging in community projects. They can actively participate in reforestation projects by organizing family outings to plant native trees and plants. This annual activity of planting at least five native plants can instill a sense of responsibility towards the environment in children. Furthermore, parents can support sustainable agriculture by participating in initiatives that promote eco-friendly farming practices. This could include volunteering at local farms or supporting community-supported agriculture programs. Through these actions, parents demonstrate the importance of sustainable land use, guiding their family towards becoming responsible Earthizens.*

*Kids: Children, with their boundless energy and curiosity, can be champions of reducing paper usage and avoiding products that harm wildlife. They can participate in monthly actions that promote paper reduction, such as using digital tools for schoolwork or creating crafts from recycled materials. These activities help children understand and appreciate the impact of their choices on the environment. Additionally, kids can avoid products that harm wildlife by learning about eco-friendly alternatives and encouraging their peers to make sustainable choices. These experiences teach children the value of protecting wildlife and instill a sense of responsibility towards creating a sustainable society.*

*Family Activities: As a cohesive unit, families can engage in activities that promote awareness about endangered species and reduce pesticide use. Monthly sessions where the family discusses the importance of protecting endangered species and the impact of pesticides on the environment can be enlightening. These discussions, facilitated by parents or elders, can involve interactive activities like quizzes or debates to make learning engaging for kids. Supporting initiatives that reduce pesticide use is another area where families can contribute collectively. Monthly actions such as using natural pest control methods or supporting organic farming help raise awareness and promote sustainable practices within the community.*

*Collective Advocacy: Families can advocate for protected areas by participating in campaigns that highlight the importance of conserving natural habitats. This could involve writing letters to local representatives or joining advocacy groups that work towards establishing and maintaining protected areas. By engaging in these activities together, families reinforce the values of conservation and sustainability. Promoting awareness about endangered species within the family, educating about biodiversity, and supporting wildlife conservation initiatives are foundational steps in this journey. Each family member, from elders to kids, contributes uniquely to these efforts, creating a ripple effect that extends beyond the household.*

*The Path to Earthizenship: The journey from homizen to earthizen is marked by a series of transformative actions that align with the Earthizens Revolution 2050. By planting native trees and plants, families cultivate a culture of environmental stewardship and responsibility. Supporting wildlife conservation and participating in reforestation projects instills a deep sense of commitment to preserving natural habitats. Advocating for protected areas and educating about biodiversity empowers families to be active participants in their communities. Reducing paper usage, avoiding products that harm wildlife, and supporting sustainable agriculture foster a sense of global Earthizenship and responsibility.*

*As families engage in these acts, they transition from being homizens—citizens of their homes—to Earthizens, proactive global citizens committed to sustainability and conservation. This transformation is not just about individual actions but about fostering a collective mindset that aligns with global sustainability and conservation. By embracing these practices, families contribute to protecting and restoring life on land, ultimately achieving the vision of a harmonious and sustainable world.*

*In summary, the journey from homizen to earthizen is a transformative process that involves every family member. Elders provide wisdom and guidance, parents advocate and engage in community activities, and children champion sustainable practices and wildlife protection. Together, families educate about biodiversity, reduce pesticide use, and advocate for protected areas. Through these collective efforts, homizens evolve into Earthizens, contributing to a sustainable and harmonious world. This journey is a call to action for families to unite and create a better future for all.*

Goal 15: Life on Land

| Act | Measurement Metric | Frequency | Target |
| --- | --- | --- | --- |
| Plant native trees and plants | Number of plants | Annually | 5 plants/year |
| Support wildlife conservation | Number of initiatives supported | Annually | 1 initiative/year |
| Reduce paper usage | Amount of paper reduced | Monthly | 10% reduction/month |
| Educate about biodiversity | Number of sessions | Monthly | 1 session/month |
| Avoid products that harm wildlife | Number of products avoided | Monthly | 5 products/month |
| Participate in reforestation projects | Number of projects | Annually | 1 project/year |
| Advocate for protected areas | Number of advocacy actions | Quarterly | 1 action/quarter |
| Reduce pesticide use | Amount of pesticides reduced | Monthly | 10% reduction/month |
| Support sustainable agriculture | Number of initiatives supported | Annually | 1 initiative/year |
| Promote awareness about endangered species | Number of awareness actions | Quarterly | 1 action/quarter |

### Goal 16: Peace, Justice, and Strong Institutions

1. Promote non-violent conflict resolution.
2. Educate about human rights.
3. Support local justice initiatives.
4. Advocate for transparent governance.
5. Participate in community decision-making.
6. Promote inclusivity and diversity.
7. Volunteer with organizations promoting peace.
8. Educate about the importance of strong institutions.
9. Support anti-corruption measures.
10. Advocate for access to justice for all.

*In the transformative journey from homizen to earthizen, each family member plays a pivotal role in embracing Sustainable Development Goal 16: Peace, Justice, and Strong Institutions. This journey is not just about individual actions but about fostering a collective mindset that aligns with global sustainability and justice. By engaging in specific acts, families can contribute significantly to creating a peaceful, just, and strong society, ultimately transforming into proactive Earthizens.*

*Elders: Elders in the family are the torchbearers of wisdom and experience. They can lead the way in promoting non-violent conflict resolution by sharing their life lessons and mediating disputes within the family. For instance, grandparents can resolve conflicts between siblings or cousins by encouraging open dialogue and understanding. This monthly practice of resolving at least two conflicts can instill the values of peace and empathy in younger family members. Additionally, elders can educate the family about human rights through monthly sessions, discussing historical events and the importance of justice and equality. Their stories and insights can provide a rich context for understanding the significance of human rights in today's world.*

*Parents: Parents are the pillars of advocacy and community engagement. They can actively participate in promoting transparent governance by attending quarterly community meetings and advocating for policies that ensure accountability. By involving themselves in these meetings, parents set a powerful example for their children on the importance of civic engagement. Furthermore, parents can support local justice initiatives by participating in annual events or campaigns aimed at improving the justice system. This could include volunteering at legal aid clinics or supporting organizations that work towards judicial reform. Through these actions, parents demonstrate the importance of justice and fairness, guiding their family towards becoming responsible Earthizens.*

*Kids: Children, with their boundless energy and curiosity, can be champions of inclusivity and diversity. They can participate in monthly actions that celebrate different cultures and backgrounds, such as organizing multicultural events at school or joining clubs that promote diversity. These activities help children understand and appreciate the richness of cultural diversity, fostering a sense of global Earthizenship. Additionally, kids can volunteer with peace organizations alongside their parents, dedicating a few hours each quarter to activities like community clean-ups or peace marches. These experiences teach children the value of working together for a common cause and instill a sense of responsibility towards creating a peaceful society.*

*Family Activities: As a cohesive unit, families can engage in activities that educate about strong institutions. Monthly sessions where the family discusses the role of institutions like schools, hospitals, and governments in maintaining societal order can be enlightening. These discussions, facilitated by parents or elders, can involve interactive activities like quizzes or debates to make learning engaging for kids. Supporting anti-corruption measures is another area where families can contribute collectively. Quarterly actions such as signing petitions against corruption or attending workshops on ethical practices help raise awareness and promote integrity within the community.*

*Collective Advocacy: Families can advocate for access to justice by participating in campaigns that highlight the importance of fair legal systems. This could involve writing letters to local representatives or joining advocacy groups that work towards ensuring everyone has access to legal resources. By engaging in these activities together, families reinforce the values of justice and equality. Promoting non-violent conflict resolution within the family, educating about human rights, and supporting local justice initiatives are foundational steps in this journey. Each family member, from elders to kids, contributes uniquely to these efforts, creating a ripple effect that extends beyond the household.*

*The Path to Earthizenship: The journey from homizen to earthizen is marked by a series of transformative actions that align with the Earthizens Revolution 2050. By promoting non-violent conflict resolution, families cultivate a culture of peace and understanding. Educating about human rights and supporting local justice initiatives instills a deep sense of justice and fairness. Advocating for transparent governance and participating in community decision-making empowers families to be active participants in their communities. Promoting inclusivity and diversity, volunteering with peace organizations, and educating about strong institutions foster a sense of global Earthizenship and responsibility.*

*As families engage in these acts, they transition from being homizens—citizens of their homes—to Earthizens, proactive global citizens committed to sustainability and justice. This transformation is not just about individual actions but about fostering a collective mindset that aligns with global sustainability and justice. By embracing these practices, families contribute to building a peaceful, just, and strong society, ultimately achieving the vision of a harmonious and sustainable world.*

*In conclusion, the journey from homizen to earthizen is a transformative process that involves every family member. Elders provide wisdom and guidance, parents advocate and engage in community activities, and children champion inclusivity and diversity. Together, families educate about strong institutions, support anti-*

*corruption measures, and advocate for access to justice. Through these collective efforts, homizens evolve into Earthizens, contributing to a sustainable and harmonious world. This journey is not just a vision but a call to action for families to unite and create a better future for all.*

Goal 16: Peace, Justice, and Strong Institutions

| Act | Measurement Metric | Frequency | Target |
|---|---|---|---|
| Promote non-violent conflict resolution | Number of conflicts resolved | Monthly | 2 conflicts/month |
| Educate about human rights | Number of sessions | Monthly | 1 session/month |
| Support local justice initiatives | Number of initiatives supported | Annually | 1 initiative/year |
| Advocate for transparent governance | Number of advocacy actions | Quarterly | 1 action/quarter |
| Participate in community decision-making | Number of meetings attended | Quarterly | 1 meeting/quarter |
| Promote inclusivity and diversity | Number of actions | Monthly | 2 actions/month |
| Volunteer with peace organizations | Number of hours | Quarterly | 5 hours/quarter |
| Educate about strong institutions | Number of sessions | Monthly | 1 session/month |
| Supporting anti-corruption measures | Number of actions | Quarterly | 1 action/quarter |
| Advocate for access to justice | Number of advocacy actions | Quarterly | 1 action/quarter |

### *Goal 17: Partnerships for the Goals*

*1. Collaborate with local organizations.*
*2. Participate in community projects.*
*3. Support global development initiatives.*
*4. Educate about the importance of partnerships.*

*5. Advocate for international cooperation.*
*6. Share resources and knowledge.*
*7. Promote volunteerism.*
*8. Support fair trade.*
*9. Participate in global awareness campaigns.*
*10. Foster partnerships within the community.*

*Each family member plays a pivotal role in embracing Sustainable Development Goal 17: Partnerships for the Goals. This journey from homizen to earthizen is not just about individual actions but about fostering a collective mindset that aligns with global cooperation and sustainability. By engaging in specific acts, families can contribute significantly to building strong partnerships, ultimately transforming into proactive Earthizens.*

*Elders: Elders in the family are the torchbearers of wisdom and experience. They can lead the way in fostering community partnerships by collaborating with local organizations. For instance, grandparents can initiate annual collaborations with local charities or community centers, sharing their knowledge and resources to support various initiatives. This practice of forming at least two collaborations annually can instill the values of cooperation and mutual support in younger family members. Additionally, elders can educate the family about the importance of partnerships through monthly sessions, discussing historical examples of successful collaborations and the benefits of working together. Their stories and insights can provide a rich context for understanding the significance of partnerships in achieving global goals.*

*Parents: Parents are the pillars of advocacy and community engagement. They can actively participate in promoting international cooperation by attending quarterly community meetings and advocating for policies that encourage global collaboration. By involving themselves in these meetings, parents set a powerful example for their children on the importance of civic engagement and international solidarity. Furthermore, parents can support global development initiatives by participating in annual events or campaigns aimed at improving global cooperation. This could include volunteering for international aid organizations or supporting initiatives that promote sustainable development worldwide. Through these actions, parents demonstrate the importance of global partnerships, guiding their family towards becoming responsible Earthizens.*

*Kids: Children, with their boundless energy and curiosity, can be champions of volunteerism and fair trade. They can participate in monthly actions that promote fair trade, such as organizing school events that highlight the importance of buying fair trade products or joining clubs that advocate for ethical consumerism. These activities help children understand and appreciate the impact of their choices on global trade and sustainability. Additionally, kids can volunteer alongside their parents, dedicating a few hours each quarter to activities like community clean-ups or charity events. These experiences teach children the value of working together for a common cause and instill a sense of responsibility towards creating a cooperative society.*

*Family Activities: As a cohesive unit, families can engage in activities that educate about partnerships. Monthly sessions where the family discusses the role of partnerships in achieving global goals can be enlightening. These discussions, facilitated by parents or elders, can involve interactive activities like quizzes or debates to make learning engaging for kids. Sharing resources and knowledge is another area where families can contribute collectively. Monthly actions such as donating books, clothes, or other resources to local organizations help raise awareness and promote the spirit of sharing within the community.*

*Collective Advocacy: Families can advocate for international cooperation by participating in campaigns that highlight the importance of global partnerships. This could involve writing letters to local representatives or joining advocacy groups that work towards fostering international collaboration. By engaging in these activities together, families reinforce the values of cooperation and solidarity. Promoting volunteerism within the family, educating about partnerships, and supporting global development initiatives are foundational steps in this journey. Each family member, from elders to kids, contributes uniquely to these efforts, creating a ripple effect that extends beyond the household.*

*The Path to Earthizenship: The journey from homizen to earthizen is marked by a series of transformative actions that align with the Earthizens Revolution 2050. By collaborating with local organizations, families cultivate a culture of cooperation and mutual support. Participating in community projects and supporting global development initiatives instills a deep sense of global responsibility and solidarity. Advocating for international cooperation and educating about partnerships empowers families to be active participants in their communities. Promoting volunteerism, supporting fair trade, and fostering community partnerships foster a sense of global Earthizenship and responsibility.*

*As families engage in these acts, they transition from being homizens—citizens of their homes—to Earthizens, proactive global citizens committed to sustainability and cooperation. This transformation is not just about individual actions but about fostering a collective mindset that aligns with global cooperation and sustainability. By embracing these practices, families contribute to building strong partnerships, ultimately achieving the vision of a harmonious and sustainable world.*

*In conclusion, the journey from homizen to earthizen is a transformative process that involves every family member. Elders provide wisdom and guidance, parents advocate and engage in community activities, and children champion volunteerism and fair trade. Together, families educate about partnerships, share resources and knowledge, and advocate for international cooperation. Through these collective efforts, homizens evolve into Earthizens, contributing to a cooperative and harmonious world. This journey is not just a vision but a call to action for families to unite and create a better future for all.*

Goal 17: Partnerships for the Goals

| Act | Measurement Metric | Frequency | Target |
|---|---|---|---|
| Collaborate with local organizations | Number of collaborations | Annually | 2 collaborations/year |
| Participate in community projects | Number of projects | Annually | 2 projects/year |
| Support global development initiatives | Number of initiatives supported | Annually | 1 initiative/year |
| Educate about partnerships | Number of sessions | Monthly | 1 session/month |
| Advocate for international cooperation | Number of advocacy actions | Quarterly | 1 action/quarter |
| Share resources and knowledge | Number of resources shared | Monthly | 2 resources/month |
| Promote volunteerism | Number of volunteer hours | Quarterly | 5 hours/quarter |
| Support fair trade | Amount spent | Monthly | ₹500/month |
| Participate in global awareness campaigns | Number of campaigns | Annually | 2 campaigns/year |
| Foster community partnerships | Number of partnerships | Annually | 2 partnerships/year |

*More towards Goal 17 :*

Partnerships for the Goals is crucial for achieving the Sustainable Development Goals (SDGs) as it emphasizes the importance of collaboration and collective action. By fostering partnerships, we can leverage diverse resources, expertise, and perspectives to address global challenges more effectively. For instance, collaborating with local organizations can enhance community resilience and drive sustainable development at the grassroots level. Setting a target of two collaborations per year ensures consistent engagement and impact.

Participating in community projects, such as environmental clean-ups or educational programs, helps build strong local networks and promotes a sense of shared responsibility. Supporting global development initiatives, like funding renewable energy projects, demonstrates a commitment to broader international goals. Educating about partnerships through monthly sessions raises awareness and equips individuals with the knowledge to form effective alliances.

By tracking these metrics, we can measure progress and ensure that our efforts as homizens contribute effectively to becoming earthizens, ultimately achieving the SDGs. Partnerships are the backbone of sustainable development, and Goal 17 underscores their indispensable role in creating a better world for all.

These matrices will help us track and measure progress towards each goal, ensuring that the efforts of homizens contribute effectively to becoming earthizens and achieving the SDGs.

These daily acts can be tracked and measured to ensure progress towards a more sustainable future. By integrating these practices into daily life, homizens can effectively contribute to achieving the SDGs and become true earthizens.

# SECTION G

# Exploring Re-imagined FUTURE

## Earthizens Revolution 2050

The Earthizens Revolution 2050 is a bold and necessary initiative to unite global efforts towards sustainability and resilience. By enrolling in this mission, university strategy teams will play a pivotal role in re-imagining the path to achieving the SDGs and shaping a better future for all.

We strongly believe that Earth is our heaven, more like our first heaven that we recollect visiting, where we play our part to make the most of what it has to offer. Perhaps only then, and maybe only after that, we may be entitled to move on to other heavens, as many believers hold.

The good, bad, and ugly experiences may make Earth appear less heavenly, which we truly understand. We believe this often happens due to situations created by a few to benefit themselves and may not particularly be to hurt others. Alternatively, it could be reasons directing an exit from this heaven, which may not align with the desires of those who are well-settled here. Unfortunately, this comes at the cost and pain of others who are equal earthizens of this planet.

Thus, it shall always remain our collective responsibility to protect it. We must come together to address the challenges we face. Together, we have to create a sustainable and harmonious world for generations to come.

## Foundation Launch

The www.GOLA.foundation was initiated as an intrapreneurial spin-off by JGU PhD student Ashish Ash Gulati, along with his equal partner, friend of 45 years, guide, and their family's CFO, Malini Ash Gulati, on National Unity Day, October 31, 2024. It is set to evolve into a couplepreneurial venture, leveraging the combined energies of both genders for its growth and progress.

The foundation is responsible for the web address www.citizen.earth and is proposed to be headed by NINE happily married global couples with Indian values, each with the experience of parenting two or more children, including at least one girl. The plan of action post the pilot phase ending in 2036 will be collectively devised by this 18-member founding team, or their nominees. This approach emphasizes gender diversity and values the unique perspectives of homemakers, ensuring visible and effective inclusivity.

## Vision, Mission and Goals

### *Vision:*

*~ The Earthizens Revolution 2050 is a comprehensive blueprint designed to foster a global community of Earthizens—inhabitants of Earth dedicated to the planet's well-being and committed to Earthizenship ~*

This movement transcends environmental conservation, aiming to redefine our relationship with the Earth and each other. The revolution envisions a world where every individual, referred to as an Earthizen, actively contributes to achieving Sustainable Development Goals (SDGs). By 2050, the goal is to have at least a billion Earthizens who are not only aware of environmental issues but are also actively engaged in solutions. This transformation requires a shift in mindset, where people see themselves as integral parts of the Earth's ecosystem, responsible for its health and sustainability.

### *Mission:*

*~ The mission of the Earthizens Revolution 2050 is to empower over a billion Homizens to become Earthizens by embracing SDGs Dil Se, ensuring a thriving planet by the year 2050 while committing to Earthizenship ~*

This mission is driven by the belief that collective action and individual responsibility are key to achieving global sustainability and peace. The foundation aims to transform "Homizens" into "Earthizens" through universities and schools, inspired by the transformation brought about by the Grameen Bank in Bangladesh, which eventually earned the Nobel Peace Prize as an organization. By leveraging the power of education and community engagement, we seek to foster a sense of global Earthizenship and responsibility.

### *Goals:*

By working towards these goals, we can create a world where every Earthizen thrives, contributing to the collective well-being of our planet.

- **Empowerment through Education:** Utilize universities to educate and inspire Homizens, transforming them into Earthizens who are committed to sustainable practices and Earthizenship.
- **Recognition of Contributions:** Recognize and celebrate Homizens who make significant contributions to sustainability, elevating them to Earthizens of Eminence, exemplifying Earthizenship.

- **Sustainable Practices:** Promote the adoption of sustainable practices in homes, categorizing them as fit or fat based on their resource utilization, and fostering a culture of Earthizenship.
- **Global Earthizenship:** Foster a sense of global Earthizenship and responsibility, encouraging individuals to contribute to global peace and noble causes.
- **Research Constructs:** Further research and develop the constructs introduced by the Earthizens Revolution 2050, ensuring they are effective and scalable, and promoting Earthizenship.
- **Constitution of Earthizens:** Prepare us to unite against global threats, including alien attacks or asteroid impacts, ensuring our collective efforts are aligned and effective. Together, through Earthizenship, we can build a brighter, more sustainable and united future for all.

## Pilot Program (2028-2036)

The pilot program will enroll 300 universities from at least 24 different countries, reflecting the 24 spokes of the Ashoka Chakra in the Indian flag. This approach is distinct from following or being a follower of the top few most developed countries. This initiative will symbolize unity, inclusivity, and collective effort towards sustainability, much like the Chakra (wheel) symbolizes in our flag. It inspires us to advance the wheel of Earthizenship with enthusiasm and positivity towards sustainability.

To start with, each university will be mentored to identify and honor 10,000 "Earthizens of Eminence," individuals who demonstrate exceptional commitment to sustainability and global Earthizenship, before 2036. These records will be meticulously maintained in university libraries, serving as a testament to their contributions and inspiring future generations.

The program aims to foster a global network of universities dedicated to the Earthizens Revolution 2050. These 300 universities could further inspire 10 universities each under their mentorship to join hands and develop researchable solutions that are minimally subjective and maximally objective, enabling transparent digital audits.

This approach will enhance the quality of Homizens graduating to become Earthizens year after year. Systems, processes, checklists, and SOPs will provide the foundation for a well-documented transformation of humans into earth-nurturing Earthizens.

By leveraging the intellectual and innovative capacities of these institutions, we will drive significant progress towards achieving the Sustainable Development Goals (SDGs). The selected universities will act as hubs of excellence, promoting research, education, and community engagement focused on sustainability and resilience.

Looking ahead, this pilot program will lay the foundation for a broader movement, encouraging universities worldwide to join the mission. By 2036, we envision a thriving network of academic institutions collaborating to address global challenges. This collective effort will eventually empower billions of individuals to embrace their roles as Earthizens, contributing to a harmonious and sustainable planet.

## Constitution of Earthizens

One of the key components of the Earthizens Revolution 2050 is the creation of a Constitution of Earthizens. This constitution, powered by AI, will provide personalized guidelines for individuals (Homizens) to align their goals with those of Earthizens. These goals shall be defined by the Constituent Assembly of those 300 Universities that come together to draft the constitution of Earthizens. This constitution will be based on the SDGs and will include actionable steps for individuals to contribute to global sustainability.

## Universities Role:

Universities play a crucial role in shaping the future and can significantly contribute to the Earthizens Revolution 2050 through various means.

**Research and Innovation:** Universities can conduct research on sustainable practices, develop new technologies, and create innovative solutions to environmental challenges, including renewable energy technologies and waste management systems.

**Education and Awareness:** Universities can educate the next generation of leaders about the importance of sustainability and global cooperation through curriculum development, workshops, seminars, and public outreach programs. They have the responsibility to enroll a large number of schools, their students, and parents into this revolution.

**Community Engagement:** Universities can engage with local communities to promote sustainable practices and encourage participation in the Earthizens Revolution 2050 through community clean-up events, tree planting drives, and awareness campaigns.

**Policy Advocacy:** Universities can advocate for policies that support sustainable development and environmental protection by working with governments, NGOs, and other stakeholders to influence policy decisions and promote best practices.

The revolution is anchored by 300 global universities that act as floating members of this assembly, as we propose. These institutions shall play a crucial role in research, education, and advocacy, driving this movement forward. They collaborate on various projects, share knowledge, and develop innovative solutions to environmental challenges. Their main goal is to draft the Constitution of Earthizens, with the first draft out by 2030 and an unanimously accepted version by 2036.

## Benefits to Universities:

By enrolling in this mission, universities can help develop and implement this constitution, ensuring its effectiveness and widespread adoption. Enrolling in the Earthizens Revolution 2050 offers numerous benefits for universities:

**Global Recognition:** Universities that participate in this mission will be recognized as leaders in sustainability and global cooperation, enhancing their reputation and attracting students, faculty, and funding.

**Collaborative Opportunities:** Enrolling in this mission provides opportunities for collaboration with other universities, organizations, and stakeholders, leading to joint research projects, shared resources, and collective impact.

**Positive Impact:** By participating in the Earthizens Revolution 2050, universities can make a positive impact on the environment and society, aligning with their mission of creating knowledge and serving the public good.

**Future Preparedness:** Enrolling in this mission ensures that universities are prepared to face future challenges, whether environmental, social, or technological, including threats like asteroids and new viruses.

**Annual Conference :** Held at the end of December, this conference brings together Earthizens from around the world to share ideas, celebrate achievements, and plan future initiatives. The conference serves as a platform for networking, learning, and collaboration, fostering a sense of global community and shared purpose.

## Visibility and Recognition on WWW.CITIZEN.EARTH

The website www.citizen.earth serves as a platform to recognize and celebrate the achievements of Earthizens. Families, including individuals as part of the family, who have successfully transitioned from Homizens to Earthizens are listed on the site, providing visibility and acknowledgment of their contributions. This public recognition not only honors their efforts but also inspires others to join the movement.

## Expanding our vision

To further enhance the impact of the Earthizens Revolution 2050, additional initiatives can be introduced. For instance, educational programs can be developed to teach the younger generation about sustainable practices and the importance of the SDGs. Community projects can be launched to promote local sustainability efforts, such as urban gardening, renewable energy installations, and waste reduction campaigns.

By involving people of all ages and backgrounds, the revolution can foster a culture of sustainability that permeates every aspect of society. That includes:

**Education:** Integrate global Earthizenship and environmental education into school curriculums by promoting AI powered A.ed for teachers. Teach teachers & students about climate change, human rights, and cultural diversity from a young age. Coach them to understand how Homizens can become Earthizens.

**Community Programs:** Initiate local programs that encourage community service, cultural exchange, and environmental stewardship. Create platforms for discussions and collaborative problem-solving. Encourage transparent audits and awards to recognize and motivate contributions.

**Policy Advocacy:** Support policies that promote sustainability, equality, and global cooperation. Encourage governments to take decisive action on climate change and social justice. Link property tax to household waste management, involving RWAs, colonies, localities, and cities. Each kilogram of waste needs to be managed for a better planet.

**Technology and Innovation:** Leverage technology to connect people across the globe, share knowledge, and coordinate efforts to tackle global challenges. It is truly important to have mechanisms where humans connect directly with other humans and gain information from human intelligence, straight from the horse's mouth. Especially in an age where AI governs so much, ensuring we know the truth becomes crucial.

**Democratizing PhD Expertise:** In this era when AI is taking away jobs of knowledge workers, it's important to understand what AI cannot replace: the undocumented, non-digitized unique knowledge each individual holds through their experience, education, and personal insights. We need platforms where humans can communicate directly with other humans, not just AI, to ensure unfiltered, untampered, and unadulterated responses.

We need setups where information is available straight from the horse's mouth.

While this might be expensive, with millions of PhD holders, why can't solutions be discussed over voice, providing unfiltered answers straight from the horse's mouth of those with PhDs, benefiting others?

We see an opportunity here for faculty members and individuals with real experiences to be heard, respected for their insights and advice, and to share their real-life experiences, which are non-digitized and inaccessible to AI. As a foundation, we aim to contribute to this space and will do our best to provide platforms that are truly non-AI, delivering insights straight from the horse's mouth, driven by the earthy hearts and minds of the experts.

With that, the Earthizens Revolution 2050 calls for increased global collaboration. NGOs, companies, governments, and private sector organizations can work together to create policies and initiatives that support the SDGs while fostering entrepreneurial ventures with an XYZpreneurial mindset. International partnerships can be formed to share knowledge, resources, and best practices for sustainable enterprises. By working together, we can create a more sustainable and equitable world for future generations.

Technological innovation will play a crucial role in the Earthizens Revolution 2050. Advances in renewable energy, sustainable agriculture, and waste management can help reduce our environmental impact. AI and data analytics can be used to monitor progress towards the SDGs for each household and identify areas for improvement. By embracing new technologies, we can accelerate the transition to a more sustainable collective future.


## Declared: Earthizens Revolution 2050

The term "Earthizens Revolution 2050" is a powerful and effective statement because it emphasizes the need for individual and household-level change, promotes conscious earning and spending, and provides a clear path for evolution to Earthizens. The revolution stands declared and has started on October 31, 2024, and we shall handhold it until it reaches its full potential.

The success of the Earthizens Revolution hinges on the actions of individuals within their households. It is more than just a movement; it is a call to action for every person on the planet. By making mindful choices in how we earn, spend, and live, we can collectively drive significant progress towards the Sustainable Development Goals (SDGs). This revolution stands declared and empowers each of us to take responsibility for our impact on the planet and contribute to a better future for all.

To conclude, this is a bold and visionary movement that seeks to transform our world by fostering a global community of Earthizens. By embracing the XYZpreneurial mindset and actively working towards sustainable development goals, we can safeguard our planet for future generations.

This revolution calls for collective action, where every individual plays a part in creating a sustainable future. Together, with the support of 300 Global Universities, we can achieve our goal.

# JOIN THE REVOLUTION AND BE PART OF THE CHANGE FROM HOMIZENS TO EARTHIZENS!

## References


Gulati, A. A. (1990-2023). Maths Revolution 2047. Delhi.

Gulati, M. &. (2024). *Sorry* (Vol. Version 3.1). Sonipat, India: Print Lobby.

Harari, Y. N. (2024). *Nexus: A Brief History of Information Networks from the Stone Age to AI*.

NETFLIX (Producer), -, N., & Stacey, N. (Directors). (2024). *BUY NOW! The Shopping Conspiracy* [Motion Picture].

Pinchot-III, G. (1985). *Intrapreneuring*. New York, USA: Harper & Row, Publishers, Inc.

# APPENDICES

## A : POLO Strategy for Sustainability

*Harnessing finance & INTRApreneurship for sustainability, in established organizations*

In today's rapidly evolving business environment, sustainability has become a critical objective for organizations worldwide. Achieving sustainable growth requires a strategic approach that leverages the strengths of finance and intrapreneurship. This essay explores the "Polo Strategy" for sustainable growth, where finance professionals and all employees adopt an intrapreneurial mindset to drive sustainability initiatives. The analogy of polo, a sport that demands coordination, strategy, and balance, serves as a powerful metaphor for this approach.

### The Strategic Role of Finance in Sustainability

Finance departments are the backbone of any organization, responsible for managing budgets, forecasting financial performance, and ensuring efficient resource allocation. However, their role in sustainability extends beyond traditional financial stewardship. Finance professionals must strategically integrate sustainability into their financial planning and decision-making processes. This involves identifying opportunities for sustainable investments, developing green financial products, and advocating for policies that promote environmental and social responsibility.

### Intrapreneurship: Driving Innovation from Within

Intrapreneurship refers to the practice of acting like an entrepreneur within an existing organization. It involves taking initiative, being innovative, and driving change from within. For sustainable growth, this mindset must permeate the entire organization. Every employee, regardless of their role, should think creatively about how to reduce costs, improve efficiency, and promote sustainable practices. By harnessing the collective intrapreneurial spirit, organizations can unlock new opportunities for sustainable growth.

### The Polo Strategy:

### A Metaphor for Sustainable Intrapreneurial Growth

The game of polo provides a compelling analogy for the strategic approach needed to achieve sustainable growth. In polo, success depends on the harmonious collaboration between the horse rider and the horse. The rider must skillfully guide the horse, making quick decisions and adapting to changing circumstances. Similarly, achieving sustainable growth requires a coordinated effort between professionals having access to financial decisions and the other employees, each playing their part in driving sustainability initiatives.

1. **The Horses**: Sustainability Initiatives

In polo, the horse's strength, agility, and endurance are crucial. In the context of sustainability, these qualities are embodied in various initiatives such as renewable energy projects, waste reduction programs, and sustainable supply chain practices. These initiatives are the foundation upon which sustainable success is built.

2. **The Players**: Finance Professionals and Employees

Just as polo players must be skilled and strategic, finance professionals and all employees must possess a deep understanding of both their roles and sustainability issues. They must be able to identify and evaluate opportunities to reduce costs, improve efficiency, and integrate sustainability into their daily tasks. This collective effort is essential for achieving the organization's sustainability goals.

3. **The Game**: Strategic Balance

In polo, the horse rider must balance control and freedom, guiding the horse while allowing it to perform at its best. Similarly, achieving sustainable growth requires a strategic balance between profitability and sustainability. This involves making informed decisions that consider both financial performance and environmental impact, ensuring that the intrapreneurial organization thrives in the long term.

*Implementing the Polo Strategy*

To implement the Polo Strategy for sustainable growth, organizations must foster a culture of intrapreneurship and strategic thinking. This involves:

- **Empowering Employees:** Encourage all employees to take ownership of sustainability initiatives. Provide training and resources to help them understand the financial and environmental impacts of their actions. This empowers the intrapreneurial team to drive sustainability forward.
- **Integrating Sustainability into Financial Planning:** Professionals having financial responsibilities should incorporate sustainability metrics into their financial planning and reporting processes. This includes evaluating the long-term benefits of sustainable investments and considering the environmental impact of financial decisions. The horse rider must use one hand to save and one hand to spend wisely.
- **Promoting Collaboration:** Foster collaboration between different departments to ensure that sustainability initiatives are aligned with the organization's overall strategy. Encourage cross-functional teams to work

together on sustainability projects, embodying the spirit of an intrapreneurial team.

- **Innovating for Sustainability:** Encourage innovation by providing a platform for employees to share their ideas for sustainable practices. Recognize and reward those who contribute to the organization's sustainability goals. This further strengthens the intrapreneurial team.

By emphasizing the roles of the horse for sustainability, the horse rider as the finance team with one hand to save and one hand to spend, and fostering an intrapreneurial team, organizations can effectively implement the Polo Strategy for sustainable growth.

## Comparing with Other Sports

To further illustrate the concept, we can compare the Polo Strategy to other sports:

1. **Football and Entrepreneurship**

Football, with its emphasis on teamwork, strategy, and quick decision-making, is a fitting analogy for entrepreneurship. Entrepreneurs, like football players, must work collaboratively, adapt to changing conditions, and seize opportunities as they arise. The dynamic nature of football mirrors the fast-paced, high-stakes world of entrepreneurship.

2. **Marathon and Solopreneurship**

The marathon, with its focus on endurance, perseverance, and individual effort, is akin to solopreneurship. Solopreneurs, like marathon runners, must rely on their own skills and determination to achieve their goals. The long, solitary journey of a marathon runner reflects the challenges faced by solopreneurs as they build their businesses from the ground up.

## Conclusion

In conclusion, the Polo Strategy for sustainable growth emphasizes the importance of strategic collaboration between finance professionals and all employees. By adopting an intrapreneurial mindset and working together as a cohesive team, organizations can achieve sustainable growth that balances profitability with environmental and social responsibility. The analogy of polo highlights the need for coordination, strategy, and balance in driving sustainability initiatives. Just as polo players and their horses must work together to win, finance professionals and employees must align their efforts to create a sustainable future for all.

## B : Glossary of Terms

1. **Annual Global GOLA Conference:** An annual event held at the end of Dec.
2. **Biodiversity Conservation:** Efforts to protect and preserve diverse ecosystems.
3. **Carbon Footprint:** The total greenhouse gas emissions caused by an individual or organization.
4. **Circular Economy:** An economic system aimed at eliminating waste and the continual use of resources.
5. **Clean Energy:** Energy derived from renewable, zero-emission sources.
6. **Climate Action:** Efforts and initiatives aimed at combating climate change.
7. **Climate Resilience:** The ability to adapt to and recover from climate-related impacts.
8. **Community Engagement:** Involving local communities in decision-making and development processes.
9. **Conscious Consumption:** Emphasizing mindful spending and supporting sustainable products.
10. **Constituent Assembly of Universities:** A group of 300 global universities leading the Earthizens Revolution.
11. **Constitution of Earthizens:** A framework for Earthizens to align with sustainable goals.
12. **Constitution of Homizens:** Guidelines for Homizens to transition to Earthizens.
13. **Corporate Social Responsibility (CSR):** Business practices involving initiatives that benefit society.
14. **Deforestation:** The clearing of trees, transforming a forest into cleared land.
15. **Earthizens:** Conscious global citizens committed to sustainability.
16. **Earthizens Day – Oct 31:** A global event uniting people in their commitment to the planet.
17. **Earthizens Revolution 2050:** A movement aiming to transform a billion Homizens into Earthizens by 2050.
18. **Earthizens of Eminence:** Individuals recognized for significant contributions to sustainability.
19. **Earthizenship:** The state of being an Earthizen, embracing global responsibility.
20. **Earthy:** Someone who truly embraces the opportunity of being on this earth, without the fear of not being here someday.
21. **Ecosystem Services:** Benefits provided by ecosystems to humans, such as clean water and air.
22. **Environmental Impact Assessment (EIA):** A process to evaluate the environmental effects of a proposed project.
23. **EYD – Estimated Year of Departure:** Estimating and declaring an imaginary year till when one believes they may be alive on planet Earth.
24. **Forent:** New coined word by author to acknowledge being a parent founder.
25. **FiT~ FaT Homes:** Homes categorized as fit or fat based on their resource utilization.
26. **Floating Members:** Universities that are part of the Constituent Assembly of Universities.

27. **Global Earthizenship:** The concept of being a responsible and proactive citizen of the world.
28. **GOLA:** Refers to Earth, inspired by movies like Prithvi, Paani, PK, Taare Z Par etc.
29. **Green Building:** Construction practices that create environmentally responsible and resource-efficient buildings.
30. **Greenwashing:** Superficial or misleading claims about the sustainability of products or practices.
31. **Habitat Restoration:** Efforts to restore natural habitats to their original state.
32. **Heaven at birth:** Embracing the opportunity of birth on Earth, as good as heaven
33. **Homizen - Copper:** The base level Homizen.
34. **Homizen - Bronze:** One level above copper level Homizens.
35. **Homizen - Silver:** One level above bronze level Homizens.
36. **Homizen - Gold:** One level above silver level Homizens.
37. **Homizen - Platinum:** One level above Gold.
38. **Homizens:** Individuals living in their homes, yet to adopt sustainable practices.
39. **Homizenship:** The state of being a Homizen, embracing responsibility and sustainable practices at home.
40. **Intrapreneurship:** Entrepreneurship within an organization, supported by the employer.
41. **Low Carbon Economy:** An economy based on low carbon power sources that minimize greenhouse gas emissions.
42. **Natural Resource Management:** The sustainable management of natural resources like land, water, soil, plants, and animals.
43. **Personalized Constitutions Powered by AI:** Constitutions tailored for individuals to align their goals with those of Homizens and/or Earthizens.
44. **Pollution Prevention:** Measures taken to reduce or eliminate the production of pollutants.
45. **POLO Strategy for Sustainability:** A strategy for sustainable growth where finance professionals and all employees adopt an intrapreneurial mindset to drive sustainability initiatives.
46. **Renewable Resources:** Natural resources that can be replenished naturally over time.
47. **S2S:** Solution to Scale, a technique proposed for humans to embrace solutions that may come across as their life's purpose.
48. **SDGs (Sustainable Development Goals):** The 17 goals set by the United Nations for sustainable development.
49. **Selfizen:** An individual who has their own constitution aligned with their home, religion, country, culture, organization, and the constitution of Earthizens.
50. **Seminal Researchable Solution:** A fresh idea that needs a lot of research and is embraced as something that hasn't been tested yet.
51. **Solopreneurship:** Entrepreneurship where the individual is the sole operator.
52. **SPFS:** Solution – Purpose – Forenting – Scale, an extension of the S2S technique.
53. **Sustainable Agriculture:** Farming practices that preserve environmental health and economic profitability.
54. **Sustainable Development:** Development that meets the needs of the present without compromising future generations.

55. **Sustainable Practices:** Practices that promote environmental sustainability.
56. Transformation Plan: A detailed plan outlining the steps and actions required to achieve a specific transformation or goal.
57. **Visionary Entrepreneurs:** Entrepreneurs who adopt the XYZpreneurial mindset.
58. **Waste Management:** The process of treating solid wastes and offering solutions for recycling items.
59. **Water Conservation:** The practice of using water efficiently to reduce unnecessary water usage.
60. **XYZ Adolescence (A.ed):** Refers to the developmental phase in the XYZ mindset.
61. **XYZ Ashram Name:** A taxonomy for sustainable entrepreneurship ventures.
62. **XYZ Believer:** A person embracing a philosophy that prioritizes the planet.
63. **XYZ Consumer:** A consumer making conscious, sustainable choices.
64. **XYZ Educator:** An educator teaching and promoting sustainable practices.
65. **XYZ Eater:** An individual choosing sustainable and environmentally friendly diets and focusing of the final set of nutrients consumed including fats, minerals, vitamins, carbohydrates, proteins etc..
66. **XYZ Employee:** An employee advocating for sustainable practices in the workplace.
67. **XYZ Investor:** An investor supporting businesses aligned with the SDGs and focused on green investing.
68. **XYZ Leader:** A leader driving sustainable initiatives and inspiring others.
69. **XYZ Mindset:** A mindset focused on sustainability and global responsibility.
70. **XYZ Producer:** A producer creating environmentally friendly products.
71. **XYZ Researcher:** A researcher advancing sustainability through innovation.
72. **XYZ preneurial Mindset:** An entrepreneurial mindset integrating sustainability and innovation.
73. **www.GOLA.foundation:** A platform supporting the Earthizens Revolution 2050.
74. **WWW.CITIZEN.EARTH:** A website recognizing and celebrating the achievements of Earthizens.

## C : Status check of words coined by author

| Word Coined by the Author | Earthizens |
| --- | --- |
| Last Date of checking availability status on World Intellectual Property Organization - https://www.wipo.int/portal/en/index.html | April 24, 2025 |
| Result from search | No Results Found |
| Decision to apply for IPR | Application filed |

Print Screen of the search done

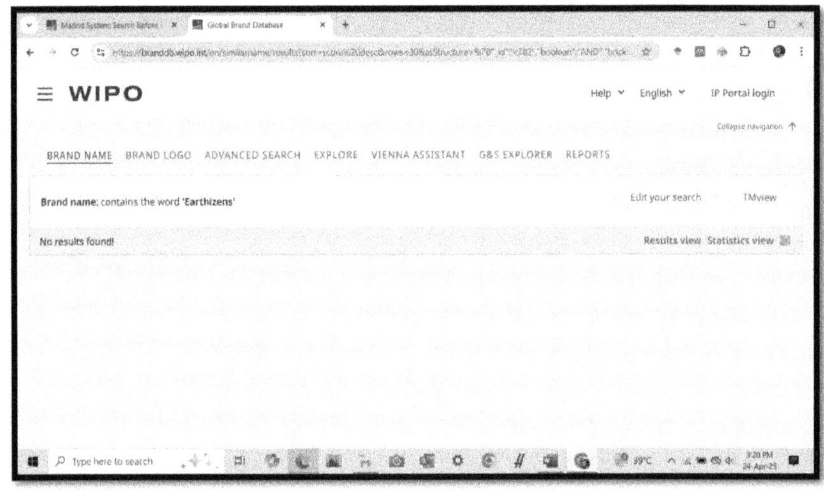


Link as shown in the URL of the result on WIPO website

https://branddb.wipo.int/en/similarname/results?sort=score%20desc&rows=30&asStructure=%7B%22_id%22:%22c782%22,%22boolean%22:%22AND%22,%22bricks%22:%5B%7B%22_id%22:%22c783%22,%22key%22:%22brandName%22,%22value%22:%22Earthizens%22,%22strategy%22:%22Simple%22%7D%5D%7D&fg=_void_&_=1745488198729

| Word Coined by the Author | Homizens |
|---|---|
| Last Date of checking availability status on World Intellectual Property Organization - https://www.wipo.int/portal/en/index.html | April 24, 2025 |
| Result from search | No Results Found |
| Decision to apply for IPR | Application filed |

Print Screen of the search done

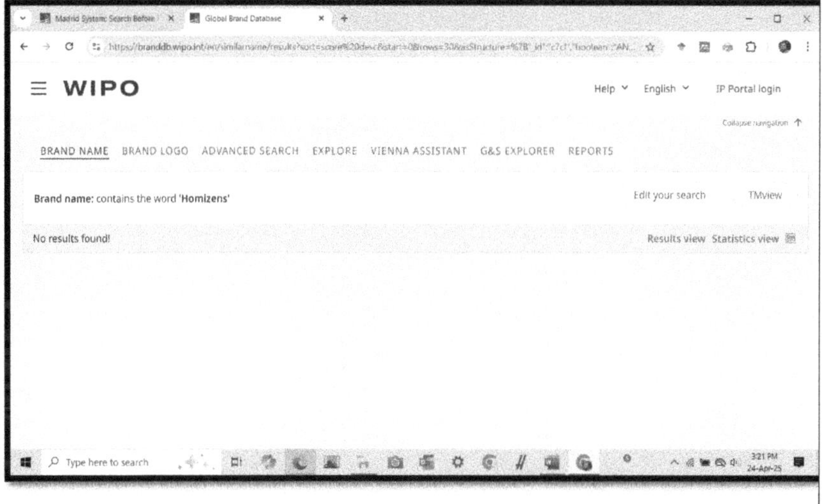


Link as shown in the URL of the result on WIPO website

https://branddb.wipo.int/en/similarname/results?sort=score%20desc&start=0&rows=30&asStructure=%7B%22_id%22:%22c7cf%22,%22boolean%22:%22AND%22,%22bricks%22:%5B%7B%22_id%22:%22c7d0%22,%22key%22:%22brandName%22,%22value%22:%22Homizens%22,%22strategy%22:%22Simple%22%7D%5D%7D&fg=_void_&_=1745488282320

| Word Coined by the Author | Earthizens Revolution 2050 |
| --- | --- |
| Last Date of checking availability status on World Intellectual Property Organization - https://www.wipo.int/portal/en/index.html | April 24, 2025 |
| Result from search | No Results Found |
| Decision to apply for IPR | Application filed |

Print Screen of the search done

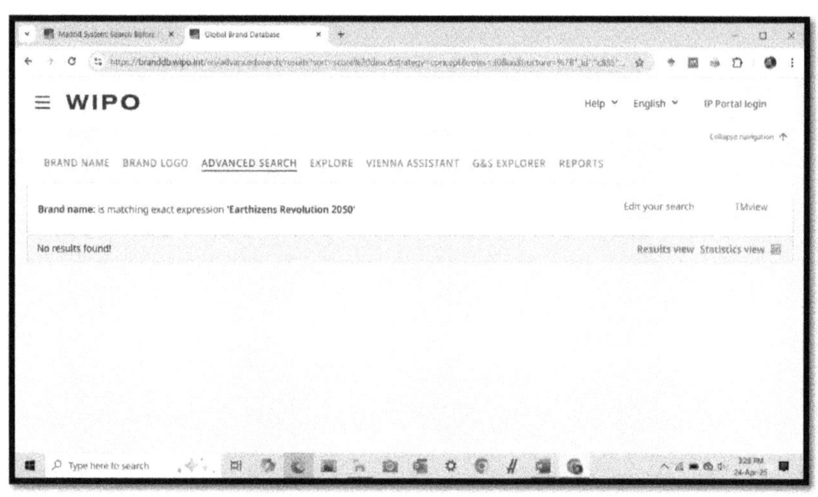

Link as shown in the URL of the result on WIPO website

https://branddb.wipo.int/en/advancedsearch/results?sort=score%20desc&strategy=concept&rows=30&asStructure=%7B%22_id%22:%22c885%22,%22boolean%22:%22AND%22,%22bricks%22:%5B%7B%22_id%22:%22c886%22,%22key%22:%22brandName%22,%22strategy%22:%22Terms%22,%22value%22:%22Earthizens%20Revolution%202050%22%7D%5D%7D&fg=_void_&_=1745488688644

| Word Coined by the Author | Earthizens Day Oct 31 |
|---|---|
| Last Date of checking availability status on World Intellectual Property Organization - https://www.wipo.int/portal/en/index.html | April 24, 2025 |
| Result from search | No Results Found |
| Decision to apply for IPR | Application filed |

Print Screen of the search done

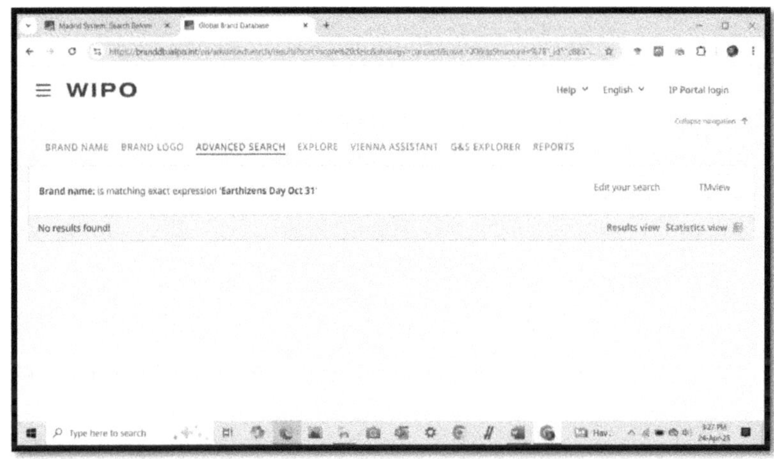


Link as shown in the URL of the result on WIPO website

https://branddb.wipo.int/en/advancedsearch/results?sort=score%20desc&strategy=concept&rows=30&asStructure=%7B%22_id%22:%22c885%22,%22boolean%22:%22AND%22,%22bricks%22:%5B%7B%22_id%22:%22c886%22,%22key%22:%22brandName%22,%22strategy%22:%22Terms%22,%22value%22:%22Earthizens%20Day%20Oct%2031%22%7D%5D%7D&fg=_void_&_=1745488635860

| Word Coined by the Author | Earthizens of Eminence |
|---|---|
| Last Date of checking availability status on World Intellectual Property Organization - https://www.wipo.int/portal/en/index.html | April 24, 2025 |
| Result from search | No Results Found |
| Decision to apply for IPR | Application filed |

Print Screen of the search done

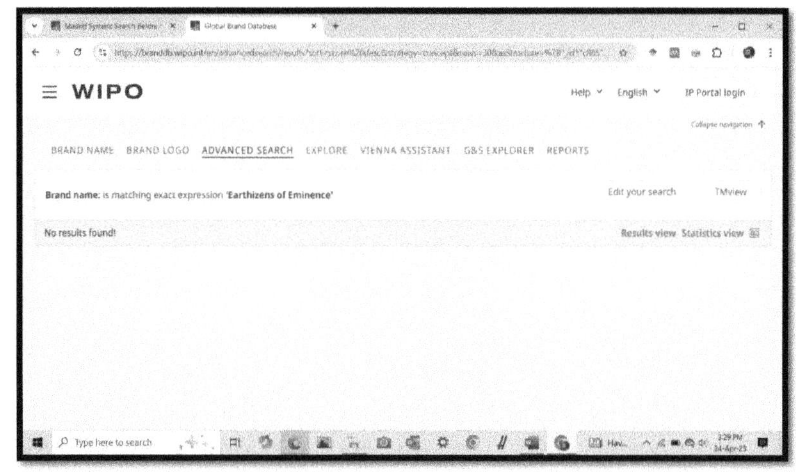


Link as shown in the URL of the result on WIPO website

https://branddb.wipo.int/en/advancedsearch/results?sort=score%20desc&strategy=concept&rows=30&asStructure=%7B%22_id%22:%22c885%22,%22boolean%22:%22AND%22,%22bricks%22:%5B%7B%22_id%22:%22c886%22,%22key%22:%22brandName%22,%22strategy%22:%22Terms%22,%22value%22:%22Earthizens%20of%20Eminence%22%7D%5D%7D&fg=_void_&_=1745488752938

| Word Coined by the Author | Constitution of Earthizens |
| --- | --- |
| Last Date of checking availability status on World Intellectual Property Organization - https://www.wipo.int/portal/en/index.html | April 24, 2025 |
| Result from search | No Results Found |
| Decision to apply for IPR | Application filed |

Print Screen of the search done

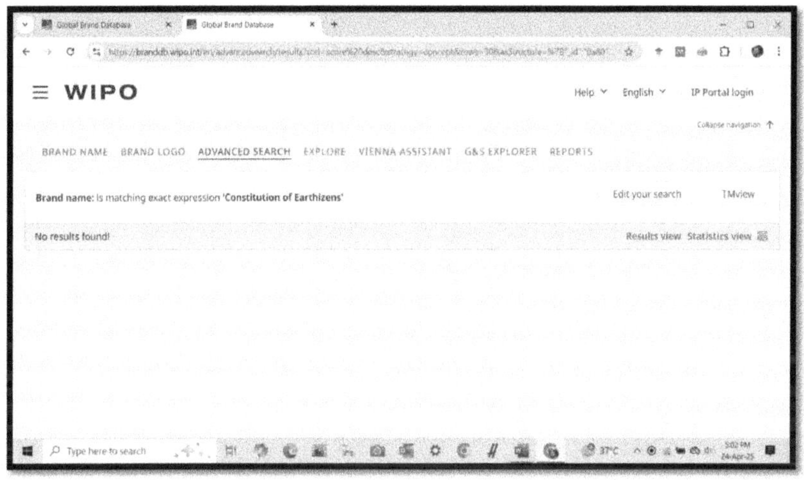


Link as shown in the URL of the result on WIPO website

https://branddb.wipo.int/en/advancedsearch/results?sort=score%20desc&strategy=concept&rows=30&asStructure=%7B%22_id%22:%220a80%22,%22boolean%22:%22AND%22,%22bricks%22:%5B%7B%22_id%22:%220a81%22,%22key%22:%22brandName%22,%22strategy%22:%22Terms%22,%22value%22:%22Constitution%20of%20Earthizens%22%7D%5D%7D&_=1745494332481&fg=_void_

| Word Coined by the Author | XYZpreneurial Mindset |
|---|---|
| Last Date of checking availability status on World Intellectual Property Organization - https://www.wipo.int/portal/en/index.html | April 24, 2025 |
| Result from search | No Results Found |
| Decision to apply for IPR | Application filed |

Print Screen of the search done

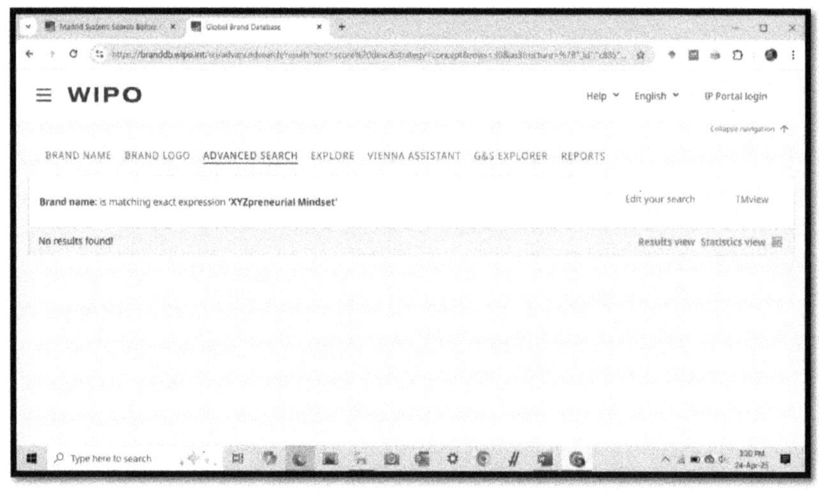


Link as shown in the URL of the result on WIPO website

https://branddb.wipo.int/en/advancedsearch/results?sort=score%20desc&strategy=concept&rows=30&asStructure=%7B%22_id%22:%22c885%22,%22boolean%22:%22AND%22,%22bricks%22:%5B%7B%22_id%22:%22c886%22,%22key%22:%22brandName%22,%22strategy%22:%22Terms%22,%22value%22:%22XYZpreneurial%20Mindset%22%7D%5D%7D&fg=_void_&_=1745488811890

| Key Word coined by Ashish Ash Gulati & Malini Ash Gulati | Earthizenship #EARTHIZENSHIP |
|---|---|
| Last Date of checking availability status on World Intellectual Property Organization - https://www.wipo.int/portal/en/index.html | April 24, 2025 |
| Result from search | No Results Found |
| Decision to apply for IPR | Application filed for the purpose of claiming to be the first person to officially give meaning to this word for global peace |

Print Screen of the search done

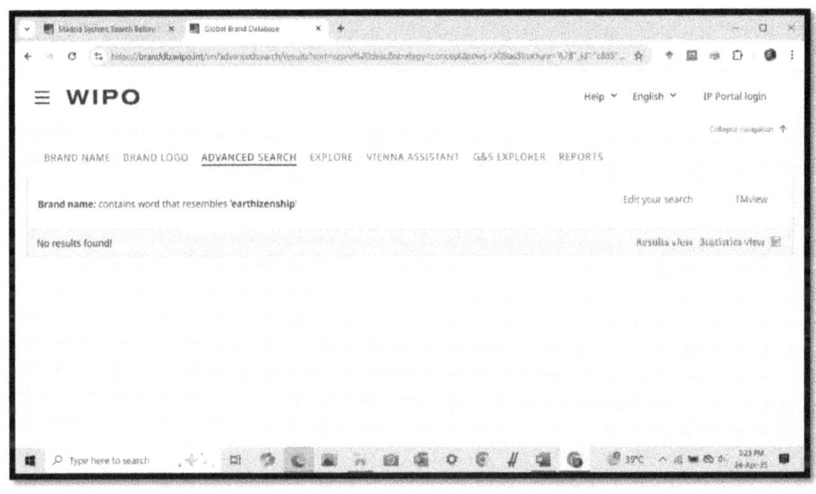

Link as shown in the URL of the result on WIPO website

https://branddb.wipo.int/en/advancedsearch/results?sort=score%20desc&strate
gy=concept&rows=30&asStructure=%7B%22_id%22:%22c885%22,%22boolean
%22:%22AND%22,%22bricks%22:%5B%7B%22_id%22:%22c886%22,%22key%
22:%22brandName%22,%22strategy%22:%22Fuzzy%22,%22value%22:%22eart
hizenship%22%7D%5D%7D&_=1745488419477&fg=_void_

https://branddb.wipo.int/en/advancedsearch/results?sort=score%20desc&strategy=concept&rows=30&asStructure=%7B%22_id%22:%22c8b1%22,%22boolean%22:%22AND%22,%22bricks%22:%5B%7B%22_id%22:%22c8b2%22,%22key%22:%22brandName%22,%22strategy%22:%22Terms%22,%22value%22:%22Earthizenship%22%7D%5D%7D&_=1745489085673&fg=_void_

Tracing the word on Google

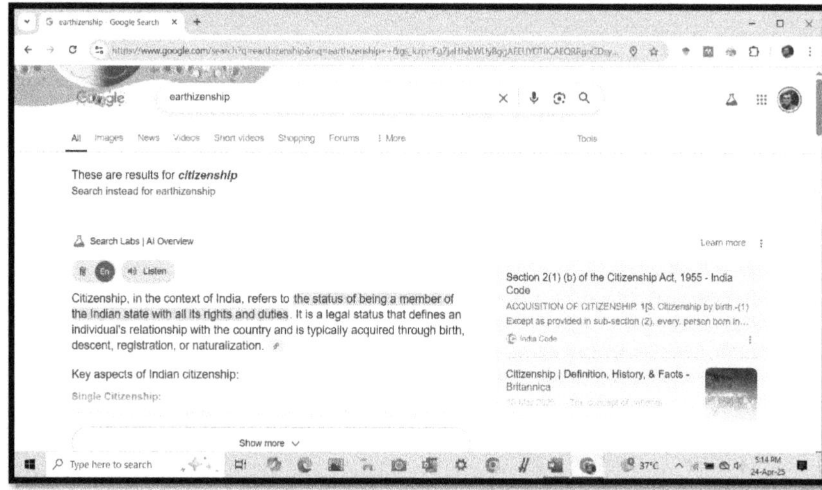

https://www.google.com/search?q=earthizenship&oq=earthizenship++&gs_lcrp=EgZjaHJvbWUyBggAEEUYOTIICAEQRRgnGDsyCQgCEAAYDRiABDIMCAMQABgNGLEDGIAEMgwIBBAAGA0YsQMYgAQyDAgFEAAYDRixAxiABDIJCAYQABgNGIAEMgkIBxAAGA0YgAQyDAgIEAAYDRixAxiABDIJCAkQABgNGIAE0gEJOTg4NWowajE1qAIMsAIB8QXySH8Go76JHA&sourceid=chrome&ie=UTF-8

~ Google does not recognize this word as on date April 24, 2025 ~

Tracing the word on Scopus Research Base

https://www.scopus.com/results/results.uri?st1=earthizenship&st2=&s=TITLE-ABS-KEY%28earthizenship%29&limit=10&origin=searchbasic&sort=plf-f&src=s&sot=b&sdt=b&sessionSearchId=fbdf6950d0a9ea05e3d03b04398c9550

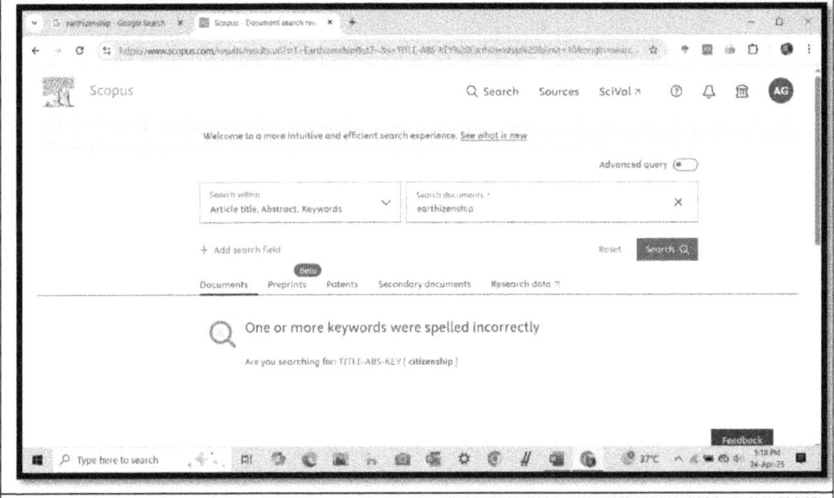

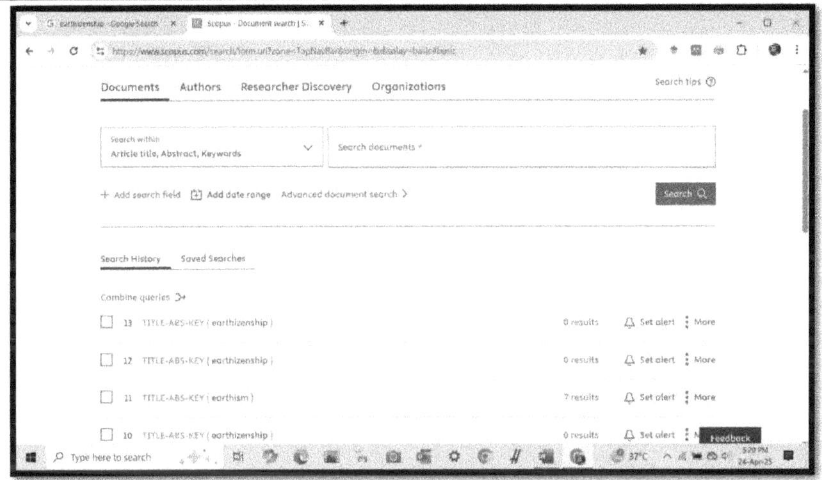

There are traces of the word Earthism seven times but there is no tracable published research paper as per Scopus with the term Earthizenship as on date April 24, 2025.

Next Validation : Copilot AI

URL Result Link:
https://m365.cloud.microsoft/chat?fromcode=bingchat&redirectid=FE5BCB8AE9624B17BDD544E82B56EAB0&auth=2&internalredirect=CCM

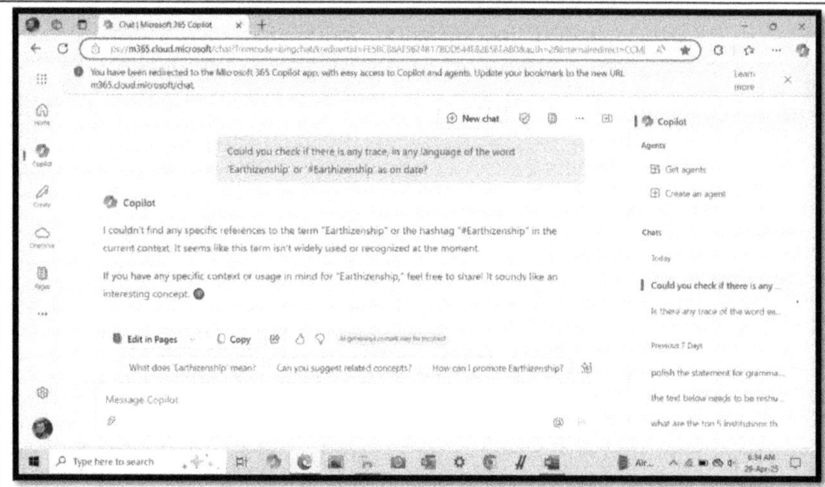

Question asked to Copilot AI: Could you check if there is any trace, in any language of the word 'Earthizenship' or '#Earthizenship' as on date?

Answer showed: I couldn't find any specific references to the term "Earthizenship" or the hashtag "#Earthizenship" in the current context. It seems like this term isn't widely used or recognized at the moment. If you have any specific context or usage in mind for "Earthizenship," feel free to share! It sounds like an interesting concept.

~ ~ ~ ~ ~

Great! We conclude that the term "Earthizenship," coined in the book Gola !?! by the author Shri Ashish Ash Gulati, life partner of Malini Ash Gulati, is a completely new term. There is no evidence of it being given any meaning before the said date, other than by the author. To verify this, the term was thoroughly searched on global databases including WIPO, Google, Scopus, and Copilot AI, and the results showing it is not in use are presented above as screenshots, as of April 28, 2025.

For this discovery, the author, as a JGU student, feels truly grateful for being inspired and occasionally mentored by Prof. Dr. C Raj Kumar (VC JGU). He believes this wouldn't have been possible without the multidisciplinary learning environment so seamlessly created for all students at O.P. Jindal Global University, Sonipat, India, through Dr. Kumar's vision and the efforts of his team.

### Congratulations, Earth!

This could mark the beginning of a new era of global peace and unity, initiated on October 31, 2024, National Unity Day of India, by Indians, from India.

# About the Author

**Malini and Ash Gulati** have been on this planet for over 50 years and feel blessed to enjoy the offerings of humanity, ensuring their time here is fruitful and lasting.

They have passed on their DNA twice, allowing future generations to carry the trace of their union. Their journey has been enriched by the fortunate parenting of Raunak and Khushi (meaning togetherness and happiness in Hindi), their two children who are now in their twenties and have completed their Bachelor of Technology degrees. As adults, they now bring forward their perspectives of Raunakology and Khushiology to the family. Additionally, Malini and Ash embrace this heaven with their adorable pet dogs, Bubbles and Cookie, who bring smiles each day.

While being parents, they supported each other in their respective higher education pursuits towards PhDs, with Malini earning the Gold Medal in her PGDM (2011-13) and Ash being recognized as the Overall Best Performer of his PT MBA batch (2015-17).

To fulfill their sincere wishes of giving further purpose to their union and contributing to this heaven in a more realistic way, they have conceptualized two revolutions: The Maths Revolution 2047 and The Earthizens Revolution 2050, which they are truly building as parents to make a larger difference someday.

Although Ashish Ash Gulati is the official author of this book, its true spirit, space, support, and personal resources were provided by Malini. Therefore, they rightfully consider each other co-authors of this second book, following their first book, *Sorry!*, which focused on the transformation plan for the Maths Revolution 2047.

Friends since age seven, they now live as a couple in Sonipat, NCR Delhi. Malini works full-time at O.P. Jindal Global University (JGU), while Ash is a part-time PhD student at JGU and a freelance social entrepreneur. This book is part of Ash's freelance spirit. Ash aims to become a full-time university faculty member in intrapreneurship, StartINs, and innovations soon. You can find them on LinkedIn as **Malini Ash Gulati** and **Ashish Ash Gulati**.

According to their own calculations and wishes, their Estimated Year of Departure is 2050 (EYD). However, due to the current wave of untimely visa cancellations and global deportation trends, they often worry about the possibility of an early or sudden departure. It's no surprise they published this book on their second proposed revolution without much feedback. The good thing is that they each serve as co-pilots for the other, making their journey of life exciting and less fearful.

April 28, 2025